INTERNATIONAL ECONOMICS

12-99

INTERNATIONAL ECONOMICS

DAVID GOWLAND

CROOM HELM
London & Sydney

BARNES & NOBLE
Totowa, New Jersey

© 1983 David H. Gowland
Reprinted 1985

Croom Helm Ltd, Provident House, Burrell Row,
Beckenham, Kent BR3 1AT

Croom Helm Australia Pty Ltd, Suite 4, 6th Floor,
64-76 Kippax Street, Surry Hills, NSW 2010, Australia

British Library Cataloguing in Publication Data

Gowland, David
   International economics.
   1. Industrial economic relations.
   I. Title
   337   HF1411

   ISBN 0-7099-1135-1
   ISBN 0-7099-1138-6 (Pbk)

First published in the USA 1984 by
Barnes & Noble Books
81 Adams Drive
Towota, New Jersey, 07512

ISBN 0-389-20438-2

Printed and bound in Great Britain
by Billing & Sons Limited, Worcester.

CONTENTS

CONTENTS

1 THE CHANGING WORLD

1.1 International Economics

In international economic text books it is conventional to start by justifying the need for a separate branch of the subject. The reason for doing so is self-evident. The whole of economics should be 'international', for example all macroeconomic analysis must take account of overseas factors. In many ways international economics is the natural extension and complement to the other branches of economics. For example, the pure theory of international trade, Chapter 2, is an extension of the elementary analysis of the gains from exchange. Commercial policy, Chapters 3 and 4, is a complement to other analyses of government intervention. Balance of payments theory, Chapters 6 to 10, extends Keynesian and monetarist analysis to an open economy and analyses the exchange rate as another macroeconomic weapon. Chapters 11 to 13, international finance, similarly complement domestic financial economics.

However, to show the value of international economics does not explain why it should be studied as a separate branch of the subject. Hence some economists have tried to find a theoretical rationale for the existence of the subject. For example, it has been suggested that within an economy all the factors of production are (perfectly) mobile but that they are not mobile between economies. From this it is natural to derive a theory of international economics as the study of the relationship between these distinct economies. Unfortunately for this approach, however, factors are not very mobile within an economy and are not immobile between them. Even labour is quite mobile between countries in many cases, e.g. the 'guest workers' from Turkey, Portugal and Italy in Germany and Switzerland and between Canada and the USA. Indeed labour is far more mobile between Michigan (in the USA) and Ontario (in Canada) than between Ontario and Vancouver or Michigan and New York.

The justification for a separate and distinct international economics is, therefore, essentially a political one. Nation states, and groupings of them, are of fundamental importance in modern life irrespective of whether different countries do or do not represent distinct economies in any theoretical sense. Thus it is necessary to study the relationships between nations and to analyse them economically because of this underlying political reality. It is equally essential to be aware of the changing nature of the world which is being studied.

1.2 Some Developments

The major change in the world economy since 1950 has been the growing interdependence of economies, especially within the developed world. Underdeveloped countries have tried to reduce their dependence and perhaps thereby contributed to their continued lack of development. This interdependence has both caused and been caused by the very rapid growth of world trade which has risen six-fold since 1950, almost twice as fast as world output (see Table 1.1). The growing interdependence of economies is dramatically revealed in the US's import ratio which was a mere 3 per cent in 1960 but nearly 11 per cent in 1980 (Table 1.1). In 1980 one new car in every four purchased in the US was an import.

This growing interdependence is in part the result of market forces. These always work to intergrate economies but their effects have been especially prominent since 1950. The most important and dramatic manifestation of market forces is the Eurocurrency market (see Chapter 13). This has produced a massive degree of integration of world financial markets and consequent integration of real markets. Real transport costs have fallen substantially, mainly because of Japanese developments in shipbuilding and the 'container revolution' they faciliated. Communications have improved dramatically because of the impact of jet planes and electronics. Innovations of all sorts, whether dramatic, like television, or humdrum, like cheaper ships, have made the world in the popular, but accurate, cliché much smaller.

This growth in world trade and increasing interdependence has been encouraged by the movement towards the liberalisation of trade, i.e. the removal of restrictions on imports. This trend in particular has meant that most countries have reduced the discriminatory taxes on imports called tariffs (see p. 28 below). In the US, for example, the average tariff was reduced from over 60 per cent in 1932 to less than 10 per cent in 1970; although this is a very crude measure of the protective effect of tariffs, it reveals the very clear trend. The high tide of protectionism was in the mid-1930s, especially after the UK abandoned free trade in 1932. The sustained trend towards liberalisation began as part of post-war reconstruction programme which also remodelled the international financial system (see p. 163 below). The moves towards trade liberalisation were originally beset with difficulty, for example no nation ratified the Havana Charter (1947) which would have set up an International Trade Organisation, ITO. Such attempts were heavily criticised, e.g. Worswick and Ady (1952), p.31, but within a decade liberalisation had become unchallenged orthodoxy: in the US after Eisenhower's Reciprocal Trade Act of 1954, in the UK after the Conservative victory in 1951. The formal framework for these developments was provided by the General Agreement on Trade and Tariffs, GATT, established in 1944 with a permanent secretariat (see Dam (1973)). In practice, barriers to trade were reduced by hard bargaining amongst national governments, e.g. in the much-vaunted Kennedy round, which was discussed from 1962-7 before implementation. The trend towards freer trade ended in the later 1970s when quasi-protectionist views became widespread in most countries.

Political developments greatly changed the environment in which world trade took place. In 1946 the British Empire and Commonwealth was still a tightly knit economic bloc comprising a quarter of the world's population. By 1970 virtually all of this former empire was independent and, while the Commonwealth survived in name, it was of economic significance only in a few areas, notably the link between New Zealand and the UK. Successor states in Africa and Asia were usually protectionist. Less dramatic and slower, but almost equal in impact, was the demise of the French Empire. China became communist in 1949 with a consequent enormous reduction in its external trade. Trade between communist Eastern Europe and the rest of the world was much less important than had been trade with its predecessors.

All of these developments had a major effect upon the pattern of world trade. An ever-increasing proportion of world trade was between members of the developed world rather than between developed and underdeveloped countries. For example, as shown in Table 1.1, only one-third of UK exports in 1951 went to Western Europe and North America, whereas by 1980 two-thirds did. Trade in manufactured goods was also of ever-increasing importance, its growth rate being over twice that of food, raw materials and fuel and amounting to around two-thirds of world trade by 1970. Hence, whereas in 1950 the typical pattern of trade was that of an underdeveloped country exchanging raw materials for the manufactured products of a developed country, by 1970 it was of two developed countries exchanging their manufactured products. These trends were reinforced by the re-emergence of

Germany as a major trading power in the 1950s. Its share of exports rose from 10 to 20 per cent of world trade in manufactured goods between 1950 and 1960. Japan also benefited. Its share of world trade rose by 50 per cent in the 1950s (from 4.1 to 6.9 per cent), nearly doubled in the 1960s and rose by over a quarter in the 1970s (see Table 1.1). The UK and USA both lost substantial shares of world trade, between them falling from nearly half of all manufactured trade in 1951 to only a quarter in 1980. This reflected many factors, some external, such as the end of the sterling area (Commonwealth) trading bloc, and some internal, especially an inability to produce cheaper reliable goods as quickly and as well as Japan.

The tendency for world trade to become ever more concentrated as trade in manufactured goods between developed countries was encouraged by the development of the EEC (European Economic Community). The origins of this were in the aftermath of World War II. On the one hand, there was a desire to ensure that France and Germany fought no more wars. On the other, there was a desire to create a strong anti-communist bloc, especially amongst the Christian Democrat politicians who were prominent in Germany, France (MRP), Italy and the Benelux countries. They were inspired by Pope Pius XII's fervent anti-communism and by Catholic social philosophy to pursue (Western) European unity. Their schemes mixed political unity, military co-operation and economic policy, e.g. in the Western European Union, and sometimes were designed to facilitate co-operation with and sometimes to exclude the USA and UK. After the defeat of the European Defence Community in 1954 and the partial eclipse of the MRP in France after 1951, the schemes became entirely economic. The first major development was the European Coal and Steel Community, ratified in 1952. However, the main changes came after the Treaty of Rome (1957) which established the EEC, or Common Market. This was a customs union (see Chapter 5) linking the six countries of France, Germany, Italy, Belgium, Luxemburg and the Netherlands. Its major achievement was the growth in trade amongst its members which the EEC stimulated both directly, by reducing tariffs, and indirectly, by promoting a favourable climate. However, its major policy was the infamous Common Agricultural Policy, CAP. This was designed to increase farmers' incomes and to reduce food imports. It utilised very high guaranteed prices and a variety of devices designed to exclude imports (see p. 66 below). The sky-high prices meant that supply of agricultural products exceeded the demand but the EEC bought up the difference and stored it, the famous butter, beef and apple mountains. The policy was enor-

Table 1.1: World Trade Patterns 1950-80

The growth of world trade

	World trade[a]	World industrial[a] production
1951	100	100
1960	161	148
1970	330	254
1980	571	343

Share of world exports of manufactured goods (%)

	1951	1960	1970	1980
UK	21.9	15.9	10.8	10.3
USA	26.6	21.7	18.5	16.9
Japan	4.3	6.9	11.7	14.8
Germany	10.0	19.4	19.9	19.8

Import ratios[b]

	1950	1960	1970	1980
USA		3.0	4.1	10.7
UK	18.0	17.8	18.0	20.6
Germany		14.7	14.9	22.2

Goods traded

1. Volume

	1948	1960	1970	1978
Food and raw materials	100	180	277	397
Fuel	100	227	302	378
Manufactured goods	100	244	560	958

2. Share (%)

	1970	1978 1970 prices	1978 prices
Food and raw materials	23.9	20.9	18.6
Fuel	9.2	7.1	16.9
Manufactured goods	65.2	69.0	63.2

1978 world prices (1970=100)

Food and raw materials	231
Fuel	620
Manufactured goods	237

UK export markets (%)

	W. Europe (of which EEC)		N. America	Overseas sterling area[c]
1951	24.5		10.7	49.5
1960	25.7		15.3	40.2
1970	37.8[d]	(21.8)	18.7[e]	36.3
1980	55.7[d]	(42.1)	11.0	

Notes: (a) Volume (b) Imports (FOB) ÷ GDP (market prices); in current prices; (c) Commonwealth less Canada plus Jordan; (d) EEC plus EFTA; (e) USA only for 1970.

Sources: IMF, *Financial Statistics;* NIESR, *National Institute Economic Review;* UN, *Statistical Year Book;* UK, US, *National Accounts;* OECD, *National Accounts Principal Economic Statistics.*

mously expensive and seemed bizarre to observers, especially as it harmed relations with the USA, Third World producers of food and other efficient farmers who disliked being excluded from European markets. However, the policy was in line with both continental tradition and Catholic social philosophy. In addition, inefficient farmers were large marginal blocs of votes in France and Germany. The UK, Denmark and Ireland joined the EEC in 1973. The decision to join the EEC was bitterly contested in the UK. Moreover, few UK politicians shared the ideals of the CAP, so there was a long series of quarrels within the enlarged EEC. The EEC was further enlarged when Greece joined in 1982.

The final important change relevant to world trade concerned the oil market. In 1965 oil prices were controlled by a group of Western oil companies, often called the Seven Sisters (Shell, BP and five US companies). They ensured that oil prices were both low and falling. This economic control was reinforced by political muscle, e.g. the Gulf sheikhdoms were still largely ruled by UK political or resident agents supported by the Royal Navy. However, in 1968, the Wilson government withdrew from the Gulf. In 1969, the pro-Western regime was overthrown in Libya and King Feisal replaced his weak brother as King of Saudi Arabia. The oil-producing countries, who had formed an organisation called OPEC (Organisation of Petroleum Exporting Countries) in 1960, were now both willing and able to stand up to the Western governments and oil companies, which they did by blocking a price cut in 1970. In 1972 they forced a small increase in oil prices. The crucial change occurred in 1973 when the price of oil was quadrupled. A further rise followed in 1978. All in all, the price of a barrel of Saudi Arabian crude oil rose from $1.80 in 1970 to $34 in 1980. Energy prices rose 520 per cent in the decade, whereas other prices rose by about 150 per cent (see Table 1.1). In value terms fuel rose from 10 to 16 per cent of world trade, although it fell in volume terms. OPEC countries acquired enormous wealth with major effects on the world financial system. Oil production was stimulated elsewhere, e.g. in the North Sea.

Note

I would like to thank Brian Hillier who read the typescript of this book and made a number of helpful comments. I should also like to thank Janet Russell who helped in various ways, especially with the bibliography.

↑

especially with a good shag on a Friday afternoon!

2 THE PURE THEORY OF INTERNATIONAL TRADE

2.1 Introduction

The purpose of the pure theory of international trade is to show why international trade exists and that it is beneficial. This might seem a redundant exercise, since there is no reason why the normal arguments used in elementary economics to demonstrate the existence of trade (internal or external) should not be applied at the international level. The argument in elementary theory is that trade will occur whenever it is profitable for two or more people to trade. If the price of a good is different in two places then it will pay someone to buy in the cheaper and sell in the dearer market. In addition to such *arbitrage* transactions, sellers will gravitate to the higher-priced market and buyers to the lower-priced until prices have been equalised. It is, in general, a sufficient condition for the existence of international trade of a good (in the absence of legal prohibitions or barriers) is that its price should be different in different countries. The gain to the participants may be regarded as self-evident or be proved using the familiar tools of welfare economics.

International trade theory, however, has set itself two slightly different and more precise goals:

1. to show that trade is beneficial to the nation as a whole, not just to exporters and importers.

This might be analysed using the 'market failure' framework to see whether international trade generates (negative) externalities but has usually been treated as a separate subject (for market failure, see Gowland (1982b), Chapter 8).

2. to show *minimum* conditions for the existence of trade.

It is easy to think of reasons for the existence of trade, such as different prices, but the theorists seek to show why prices differ and to find as many reasons as possible why they might differ. There are two principal approaches to these problems: the Ricardian and the Hecksher-

Ohlin (p. 16), besides the alternative theories reviewed in section 2.9.

2.2 The Ricardian Theory

The Ricardian, or classical, theory of international trade argued that trade would occur and would be beneficial because of *comparative advantage*. This was simply a way of saying that beneficient trade would occur if *marginal opportunity costs* differed between countries. Given competitive assumptions, different marginal (opportunity) costs will be reflected in different prices, as it is, of course, a basic prediction of competitive analysis that price equals marginal cost; so the existence of trade is guaranteed. It is desirable because it will produce a potential pareto improvement compared to autarky (no trade), i.e. that more of all goods will be available for consumption so there must be a conceivable distribution of income that will make everyone better off, the definition of a potential pareto gain. This argument is best demonstrated by an example, which abstracts and simplifies by using only two countries and two goods. The two countries will be labelled the USA and the UK; anyone not sharing this Anglo-Saxon chauvinism should relabel as 'the rest of the World'. The two commodities will be wheat and cotton, a gesture to textbook tradition. The example is shown in Table 2.1.

Without trade, the US produces and consumes 50 million bushels of wheat and 30 million bales of cotton. Its marginal opportunity cost of production of 1 million bushels of wheat is 1 million bales of cotton. In other words, for each 1 million bales of cotton by which production is reduced, 1 million extra bushels of wheat can be produced and vice versa. The UK produces and consumes 10 million bushels of wheat and 8 million bales of cotton. Its marginal opportunity cost of 1 million bales of cotton is 3 million of wheat. Hence, if it reduces production of cotton by 1 million bales, wheat output can rise by 3 million, and if wheat output is reduced by 3 million bushels, cotton output can rise by 1 million bales.

With the aid of a *deus ex machina*, perhaps the Walrasian auctioneer on his day off, the two nations decide to:

1. trade at a price of two bushels of cotton for one of wheat;
2. the US will sell 6 million bushels of cotton to the UK in exchange for 12 million of wheat;
3. the US will reduce its output of wheat by 10 million bushels and

Table 2.1: Gains from Trade

		No trade Production (= consumption)	Production	*Trade* Exports (−) Imports (+)	Consumption	Gain from trade
US	Wheat	50	40	+ 12	52	+ 2
	Cotton	30	40	− 6	34	+ 4
	Marginal opportunity cost 1W:1C					
UK	Wheat	10	25	− 12	13	+ 3
	Cotton	8	3	+ 6	9	+ 1
	Marginal opportunity cost 1W:3C					

Note: US trades 6 million bales of cotton for 12 million bushels of wheat; US reduces production of wheat by 10 and so can increase output of cotton by 10; UK reduces production of cotton by 5 and so can increase output of wheat by 15.

increase its output of cotton by 10 million bales so it will produce 40 of each;

4. the UK will reduce its output of cotton by five million bales and
increase its output of wheat by 15 million bushels — it will now
produce 25 million bushels of wheat and 3 million bales of
cotton.

The outcome is shown in Table 2.1. The US now consumes 52
million bushels of wheat (40 it produces and 12 it imports) and 34
million bales of cotton (40 it produces less 6 it exports). This represents
a gain of 2 million bushels of wheat and 4 of cotton compared to
autarkic consumption. The UK consumes 13 million bushels of wheat
(25 produced less 12 exported) and 9 million bales of cotton (3 produced and 6 imported); a gain of 3 and 1 respectively. Hence trade has
made both nations better off.

A number of crucial aspects of the analysis must now be emphasised.

2.2.1 Independence of Productivity

The example assumed nothing about productivity. There might be 200
million people in the US or just one person. Nothing in the example
would change. This reveals why a nation can be more efficient in producing both goods and still gain from trade. If the US population were
5 per cent of the UK's, it would be more efficient at producing both
goods (since it produces more of both with less resources and by examination of the marginal opportunity costs). If the US population were
five hundred times that of the UK's, the reverse would be true. In either
case the gains from trade would be the same.

2.2.2 Distribution of Income

Nothing is said in the example about who consumes the goods. It may
be that international trade produces so adverse a distribution of income
that autarky is (socially) preferable. The pro-trade argument needs to
be either indifferent to distribution or assume that income distribution
can be costlessly altered by other means, see p. 34 and p. 49 below.

2.2.3 Full Employment

The argument above implicitly assumes full employment, when wheat
production was reduced, cotton production was assumed to rise. There
was no consideration of whether this would, rather than could, happen,
or whether instead resources might be unemployed. Those arguing for
the adverse effects of trade have always concentrated on this.

2.2.4 Price

The price was plucked out of mid-air; the theory says nothing about price, except that for beneficient trade price must lie between the two marginal opportunity costs. Relative prices of exports and imports are called the terms of trade, see p. 13 below. Many Third World countries have grumbled about unfair terms of trade — and so have some European nations since oil prices rose.

2.2.5 Incomplete Specialisation

The Ricardian theory does not imply complete specialisation. In the example, both the UK and the US continue to produce both goods. For complete specialisation it would be necessary both for marginal opportunity costs to be constant and for trade to take place at the level at which it maximises welfare.

2.3 The Gains from Trade

The gains from trade can conveniently be illustrated by Figure 2.1. XY is the production possibility frontier of an economy which can produce two goods x and y; the slope of XY is therefore the marginal opportunity cost of x in terms of y. Without trade XY is also the consumption possibility frontier. Some point such as A represents the highest possible level of welfare under autarky, i.e. without trade. If this nation starts to trade, its consumption possibilities are expanded. VW is a line drawn tangential to XY (at P) whose slope is equal to the world price of x in terms of y. The nation can produce at P and then exchange along VW. Between P and V the nation would be giving up some (exporting) y and receiving (importing) x; between P and W it would export x and import y. If the nation were to export x it would receive x times the (world price x/ world price y) units of y for each unit of x it exported. As the relative price of x in terms of y is, by definition, the slope of VW, it can be checked that VW does represent the trading opportunities open to this economy.

VW also represents the new consumption possibility frontier. The nation can produce at P and trade along VW, so it can consume anywhere along VW. The gains from trade are the expanded consumption possibilities, the shaded area between XY and VW. Any point in the area SAR represents a potential pareto gain compared to A, as more of both x and y could be consumed. Some new consumption point along SR, e.g. C, would clearly leave the economy better off than at A

Figure 2.1: The Gains from Trade

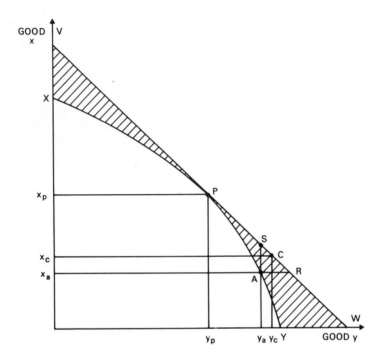

(subject to the reservations discussed in 2.2 above). Some poing along VS or RW might be superior to C but it would then be preferred to A as well. At C, this nation produces x_p and y_p and consumes x_c and y_c so it is exporting (x_p-x_c) and importing (y_c-y_p) in exchange. The gains from trade have enabled the consumption of both x and y to rise, by (x_c-x_a) and (y_c-y_a) respectively.

In this presentation it was assumed that the nation was a price taker in world trade, i.e. unable to influence the world price of x in terms of y. If this were not so, e.g. if the size of this nation's imports influenced the price, two minor changes would have to be made to Figure 2.1 since VW would be convex and there would no longer be a single optimal output P but many different Ps each associated with a point along or segment of VW. Neither of these would change the main thrust of the gains from trade argument.

2.4 The Terms of Trade

There have been various references to the *terms of trade* above, so it is useful to deal more formally with them at this point. The terms of trade are normally defined as the relative price of exports in terms of imports. When the price of imports falls, the terms of trade are said to improve. This happened to the UK in the 1930s and 1950s when the price of its imports fell very rapidly and on both occasions UK consumption per capita rose because of this. In 1973 OPEC's raising of oil prices (p. 6 above) dramatically worsened the terms of trade of oil importers such as Germany and Japan. (The UK's Terms of Trade, 1963-82 are shown in Table 2.2.)

Table 2.2: The UK's Terms of Trade (1975=100)

1963	114.9
1964	113.5
1965	116.4
1966	118.7
1967	120.3
1968	115.7
1969	115.9
1970	118.8
1971	119.8
1972	121.1
1973	106.8
1974	93.1
1975	100.0
1976	97.9
1977	100.2
1978	105.9
1979	106.3
1980	103.7
1981	101.9
1982	101.2

This measure of the terms of trade, i.e. export prices ÷ import prices, can be measured in various ways depending upon which price indices are used — e.g. wholesale prices, retail prices or GDP deflator. The usual index number problem arises when the price of some imports rises and that of other falls. If the UK used to import 10αs at 10 cents and 1β at 1\$ and now imports 1α at \$1 and 10βs at 10 cents, import prices could be said to have risen, fallen or remained unchanged.[1] However, great the practical and theoretical problems of measurement, the conceptual idea of the opportunity cost of exports in terms of imports is clear.

The above definition of the terms of trade is sometimes called the net barter terms of trade (as opposed to the gross barter terms when the *quantity* of imports is divided by the *quantity* of exports; the two measures are identical so long as exports equal imports). An alternative definition called the single factoral terms of trade seeks to measure the cost of imports in terms of home factor inputs such as labour time. For example, if an imported bottle of champagne cost an (exported) bottle of whisky in 1950 and two bottles in 1980, this definition asks how much time was needed to produce a bottle of whisky in 1950 and compares it with the amount of time needed to produce two bottles in 1980. A final definition (double factoral) compares the amount of labour used to produce both exports and imports in the two years. Despite the labour lavished by Viner, Taussig, Spraos and others on different definitions of the terms of trade, attention is almost invariably focused on the simplest − the price of imports ÷ price of exports, i.e. the net barter terms of trade.

2.5 Testing the Ricardian Theory

There are a number of major problems which render the theories of international trade exceptionally difficult to test. The first is that the predictions derived from the theories are of such a long-run nature that most conventional econometrics is irrelevant. Moreover it is very diffi-ciult to imagine, let alone quantify, the pattern of production and costs in the UK if there were no trade so as to compare it with the post-trade pattern. A simple examination of *ex post* exports and imports cannot reveal all the *ex ante* information necessary to test the theories. Finally, there are horrendous conceptual and data problems faced by any investigator in this area. The Ricardian theory in particular is very difficult to set up in a refutable fashion so that it can be tested. It is possible to describe almost any pattern of trade in a fashion consistent with the theory. Nevertheless, a number of studies have attempted to test a modified and refutable version of the theory. The pioneer was MacDougall (1951-2), followed by Stern (1962) and Balassa (1963).

MacDougall sought to find a measurable version of the 'marginal opportunity cost' concept used on p. 8 above, and to apply it to the US and UK, using data for 1937. He decided that productivity differentials were the most appropriate available measure of this, even though these were available only as *ex post* average rather than *ex ante* marginal relationships. Because of data availability he could only use labour productivity. The theory is concerned with comparative not absolute productivity, so MacDougall had to determine the average productivity differential because the US had higher productivity in all industries. Where the differential was above average, the US had a comparative advantage; where it was below average, the UK had one. MacDougall observed that US wages were about twice the UK level. This ratio would reflect the average productivity differential so long as the neo-classical (marginal productivity) theory of wages was valid. MacDougall made this assumption so that he could divide the 25 industries he was using into those in which the US had a comparative advantage and those in which the UK had one. Given the prevalence of trade restrictions he chose to examine US and UK exports to Third World countries rather than their trade with each other. In the purest case, if the US and UK competed on level terms in, say, Argentina, then the pattern of their exports should reflect the desired trade that the theory sought to explain, not the pattern that governments permitted. The pattern of trade was consistent with MacDougall's version of the Ricardian model, but the UK dominated markets where the US productivity advantage was less than 2.4 to 1 rather than 2 to 1 as he had hypothesised. This could be because of demand factors, i.e. reasons of taste or that British goods were more acceptable for political reasons. In addition British goods benefited from 'imperial preference' in some markets. Alternatively, MacDougall might have misclassified the boundary between US and UK comparative advantage.

Stern and Balassa (1963) obtained similar results using 1950 data but found that the UK had lost significant market shares to the US which suggested that the division between US and UK comparative advantage was closer to the theoretical value. This cross-section correlation between export success and productivity gives strong support to the Ricardian theory. In may seem obvious that industries with higher productivity are better able to compete internationally and so export more, but this is the Ricardian theory. The Hecksher-Ohlin model, for example, denies any role to productivity in explaining international trade.

2.6 The Hecksher-Ohlin Theory

The major rival to the Ricardian theory of international trade is the Hecksher-Ohlin theorem, which *inter alia* helped to win the Nobel Prize for Ohlin. (Both Ohlin's (1933) and Hecksher's (1919) contributions are reprinted in Ellis and Meltzer (1949).) Their work was based on the assumption, discussed on p. 1 above, that goods were mobile between countries while factors were immobile.

The argument used by Hecksher and Ohlin was that countries would like to trade factor services but were unable to do so, so they traded goods instead. Goods were traded as a method of indirectly trading the factor services embodied in them. A nation with a lot of capital and very little labour would like to import labour services and export capital ones. This was deemed to be impossible (except for special cases like Switzerland, which has always imported labour, traditionally Italian; now copied by other Western European economies). Hence the nation would export capital-intensive goods and import labour-intensive ones. In general it was argued that a nation will export goods which are intensive in the factor with which it is relatively well endowed and import the reverse case. Hence the Hecksher-Ohlin theory is often called the *factor-endowment theory* of international trade. This theory seeks to establish a minimum condition for international trade so its exponents usually rule out alternative reasons for trade by assumption – e.g. different tastes or different production functions; of course the latter is the *raison d'être* of the Ricardian theory.

The Hecksher-Ohlin theory has been subject to a lot of empirical testing which has not left it unscathed, e.g. the Leontief paradox, below. Hence it is worth emphasising that the theory is very useful in explaining trade within a firm. A large fraction of world trade is carried out within multi-national firms such as Ford or ITT and, undoubtedly, the location of factories by Ford could be explained by factor endowment, as modified by government intervention. ITT, for example, produces capital-intensive television components in California and ships them to Taiwan for the labour-intensive assembly stage.

2.7 Testing the Hecksher-Ohlin Model

The factor endowment theory has been much more extensively tested that the Ricardian theory (see Grubel (1977) pp. 62-5). The most famous and important of these studies was by Leontief (1969, originally published in 1953). Leontief was the pioneer of input-output analysis for which he was ultimately awarded the Nobel Prize. He used the US input-output matrix for 1947 to test the Hecksher-Ohlin model. Leontief calculated the factor inputs into $1 million of American exports; strictly he estimated what resources would be released if US exports were reduced by $1 million. He then calculated the inputs of factors that would be required to produce within the US $1 million of goods actually imported in 1949. Leontief regarded this as the appropriate measure of the factore-intensiveness of US imports. Thus he could compare the factor-intensiveness of US exports and imports. Moreover his methodology had created composite goods for exports and imports which represented all the goods actually traded in the correct proportions and so came as close a test of the two-good Hecksher-Ohlin model as was possible.

Leontief expected that US exports would be more capital-intensive than her imports since the US was obviously a capital-rich nation. Hence, according to the factor endowment theory, it should export capital-intensive goods and import labour-intensive ones. Instead US exports were more labour-intensive than her imports. This apparent contradiction of the predictions of the Hecksher-Ohlin model was called the Leontief paradox. There have been many attempts to explain it, either by showing that Leontief's results were wrong or by showing which of the Hecksher-Ohlin assumptions was inappropriate.

2.7.1 1947 Was an Atypical Year

This obvious comment on the results was first made by Swerling (1954). 1947 was not a typical year as economies were still recovering from World War II. However Leontief (1956) and Baldwin (1971) replicated the calculations for 1951 and 1962 respectively and still found the paradox.

2.7.2 Leontief's Results Were Not Significant

This proposition was advanced by Loeb (1954) who showed that the difference between the capital-intensiveness of US exports and imports was not statistically significant. However, the later work did find significant differences.

2.7.3 Capital Was Measured Inappropriately

This criticism was made by Buchanan (1955) who argued that Leontief had failed to take account of the different lengths of life of different capital goods. Leontief had used the capital stock to measure capital-intensiveness, not the capital services used (e.g. if good 1 were produced using £10 million of capital which lasted ten years and good 2 using £10 million of capital which lasted five years, Leontief said they were equally capital-intensive, whereas in reality good 2 is more capital-intensive). Buchanan is right but it is not clear if this mismeasurement would produce a systematic bias.

2.7.4 The Trade Pattern Reflects Protection Not Market Forces

This is another problem that arises in the real world. In 1947, the US was a highly protectionist economy. Hence *ex post* trade reflected what was permitted and possible rather than what was desired, whereas both Ricardian and Hecksher-Ohlin seek to explain desired trade. The US economy was much more open to trade by 1962 so this problem is less applicable to Baldwin's results.

2.7.5 Demand Effects

This proposition is that the US has such a differential demand for capital-intensive goods that it imports them in addition to its own production (see p. 22 below). It is plausible that the US (in 1947) was both the richest country as well as the best endowed with capital and that capital-intensive goods are highly income elastic (e.g. electricity). In this case, tastes would explain the pattern of trade, rather than factor endowments, in a pattern consistent with the Hecksher-Ohlin model. The evidence, however, does not seem to support the demand theory — Grubel (1977) says that 'it should be rejected' (p.67) and Sodersten (1979) that 'it is more of a theoretical curiosum than a very likely empirical possibility' (p.69).

2.7.6 Factor Reversals

One of the assumptions of the Hecksher-Ohlin model is that there are no reversals of factor intensity, that is that the ranking of goods by capital-intensiveness of their method of production is the same in all countries. If this assumption is not valid, the factor endowment theory collapses. There is a lot of support for this explanation of the paradox but little evidence, although it is clear that such reversals may occur (see appendix, p.25) but not that if they did it would explain the paradox.

2.7.7 US Labour Is Better

This explanation was advanced by Leontief himself in 1956. His argument is that the US is really labour rich, contrary to appearances, since each US worker is worth three workers elsewhere. Hence corrected for effectiveness the US is labour rich; rather in the vein of Sir Roger de Coverley's 'one Englishman could beat three Frenchmen . . . that London Bridge was a greater piece of work than any of the Seven Wonders of the World', and the rest of his 'honest prejudices' so gently guyed by Addison. As Leontief recognised, such a proposition is inconsistent with the simple Hecksher-Ohlin model. It is therefore useful to expand the model to bring in extra factors which may explain the superiority of American labour. The most obvious is human capital, discussed in section 2.7.8.

2.7.8 An n Factor World

This is the simplest and best way to redeem the factor endowment theory. If one extends the analysis to n factors, the US would still export goods intensive in the factor(s) with which it is well endowed but this need no longer be either labour or capital. The US is well endowed with land and natural resources and relatively well endowed compared to all but a few countries (Australia, Argentina). It exports products, like wheat, which are land-intensive but also labour-intensive. If one follows Becker's analysis of 'human capital', the US is certainly better endowed with human capital than other countries because of its expenditure on education and health. This factor is, however, embodied in US labour, so exports which are human-capital-intensive seem to be labour-intensive in a two-factor analysis.

2.7.9 Technology

The most radical departure from the factor endowment theory is to drop the common production function assumption and to argue that US technology was superior and explained its trade pattern. Such analyses are considered below, p. 22.

To summarise, the Leontief paradox may reveal the irrelevance of Hecksher-Ohlin to explaining trade patterns or it may be extended to 'n factors' and still be applicable.

2.8 The Factor Price Equalisation Theorem

Samuelson (1948) was the first to demonstrate the factor price equalisation theorem. However, it is a natural and obvious extension of the Hecksher-Ohlin theory. It is a fundamental result in elementary microeconomic theory that trade within a market leads to the equalisation of price within it, indeed it is a condition of equilibrium. As the factor endowment theorem argues that international trade is trade in factor services, albeit indirectly, the natural result would be an equalisation of their price. The stringency of the assumptions necessary to demonstrate the proposition is, therefore, more surprising than the theorem itself. Despite the apparent unrealism of the theorem, it has nevertheless been the basis of applied analysis especially within the context of the EEC, e.g. by Dosser in Shoup (1967). Before examining the factor price equalisation theorem it is important to stress that it could be proved using alternative assumptions within the framework of other models, e.g. free movement of labour in the Ricardian model.

The assumptions that are necessary to prove the FPET are:

1. perfect competition in all factor and goods markets in all countries;
2. perfect certainty;
3. the number of commodities must be at least equal to the number of factors (this can always be achieved by a redefinition of factors or commodities);
4. production functions should exhibit constant returns (empirically not unreasonable);
5. production functions should be identical in all countries.

This does not mean that the *method* of production must be the same in each country but that the same technique must be *available* to each country.

6. no reversal of factor intensities; this assumption ensures that in all countries the ranking of industries by capital intensiveness is the same, see appendix;
7. zero transport and transaction costs;
8. no externalities;
9. no total specialisation, i.e. each country must produce each good.

It is clear that these assumptions can be relaxed but not in exactly what manner. The major research into this area was pioneered by Batra (1975) and Kemp (1976). They showed that if either assumption (2) or (7) is relaxed, the FPET is valid only in the modified form, that trade reduces inequalities in factor returns rather than eliminates them.

The theorem is usually proved for two countries, one of which is relatively well endowed with capital, the other with labour; and two goods, one capital-intensive and one labour-intensive. Here the countries are C which is relatively capital-rich and L, the goods shoes (labour-intensive) and cars. The assumptions listed above ensure that for both goods in both countries price equals marginal cost and that factors are paid their marginal revenue products which are also equal to price times marginal physical product.

Wages are the same in both industries within each economy and so are profits per unit of capital, so marginal revenue products are the same in each industry. Two intuitively obvious results follow: under autarky, wages are lower and labour-intensive goods cheaper in an economy with more labour relative to capital. The labour:capital ratio is higher in L, so MRP of labour must be lower under autarky. Hence wages are lower in L than C (and capital rentals higher), given assumption (2). Marginal cost, and so price, for each industry in each country can be calculated as the sum of the marginal physical products of each factor times their price. Consequently the price of cars will be higher in L and that of shoes in C.

As shoes are more expensive and wages higher in C, trade leads to less production of shoes and more of cars in C. This reduces the demand for labour and increases that for capital in C. Therefore wages fall in C (and profits rise in L by the same argument). This continues until the prices of the goods are equalised between countries. When prices are equalised, as prices reflect marginal costs and marginal costs marginal products, the sum of the marginal revenue products must be the same in each industry across countries. This is only possible if marginal revenue products, and consequently factor prices, are equal.

2.9 Other Theories

There are a wide range of other theories of international trade besides the Ricardian and factor endowment theories. Some are implicit, or even explicit, within the two major theories. Others are extensions of them or involve manipulation of neoclassical economics. Others are overtly political or are distinctly hostile to orthodox economics or both. Some of the theories are intellectually coherent, some useful, but some are neither.

One theory which is implicitly accepted by proponents of the orthodox theories is the proposition that trade takes place because of *differences in tastes* between countries. No one denies that this could cause trade; it is for this reason that identical tastes are usually assumed so as to show that it is differential factor endowments which create the incentive to trade, not differential tastes. To take an extreme, simple example of this theory, imagine two countries with identical populations and equal GDP and factor endowments. A has a comparative advantage in producing good x so it produces 60,000,000 tons of it and B only 40,000,000. Nevertheless such is the desire of A's citizens for x that they consume 80,000,000 and B's only 20,000,000. Thus, A actually imports a good in which it has a comparative advantage because of the difference in tastes. Real world examples are hard to find. Tastes clearly help to shape the pattern of trade, e.g. UK imports of lamb and tea, but rarely determine them without the interaction of other factors. If differences in tastes are extended to include any difference in the proportion of income spent on goods, examples are easier to find, e.g. the US imports oil although it is a large producer as well. (Strictly this may not be a difference of tastes; the high US energy consumption:income ratio may reflect the level of income as much or more than taste.)

The theories that argue that international trade occurs because of *differences in technology* are really variants of the comparative advantage theory; the technological differences no doubt often explain why there are different marginal opportunity costs in the different countries. In their simplest forms, technological theories of trade are merely special cases of comparative advantage. However, more sophisticated variants claim to present a dynamic theory of trade and development. This is the *product cycle* or *imitation gap* theory associated with Kravis, Posner and Kindelberger. In the simplest case, there are three countries A, B and C, of which A is the most technologically advanced and C the least. A invents a product, x, and exports it to B and C. After a while B acquires the technology to produce x but by now A has a new discovery, y, so A exports y to B and C while B exports x to A and C. Finally, C acquires the means to produce x (and can undercut B) but B's engineers have discovered how to make y and A's inventors have a new high-technology product z. Hence each country exports one good to the other two, A exporting z, B y and C x. With the USA, Japan and Taiwan as the countries and computers, cars and textiles as the products, the story is plausible but it is not clear how generally applicable the theory is. The theory is, arguably, most useful as a reminder that comparative advantage may not persist and that a nation should not try to sustain old export industries after they have lost their cost advantage.

Kravis also pioneered another theory, the *availability* doctrine which is wrong in so far as it is not vacuous. This is that trade takes place principally in goods which are only available in one country and cannot be made or produced elsewhere. This could be interpreted as infinite comparative advantage. However, there are no such goods, barring those where the district defines the product: sherry, champagne, scotch whisky. In these instances, competition is provided by very close substitutes (Australian sherry, Asti, other grain-distilled spirits) and purchases are determined by comparative cost (and quality), not simple availability. In other cases, the theory is misleading. In one sense Kuwait and Saudi Arabia do export oil because it is available there. However it is also available virtually everywhere else in the world, the difference being one of cost. Even if oil were not available, coal (or peat) would be, or wood could be grown. Undoubtedly it would be much more costly for Japan to use alternative fuels or to obtain oil from the Tsuggru Strait. However, it is not that oil is available in Kuwait and not in Japan but that it is available in Kuwait at a minute fraction of the cost which explains why Japan imports oil.

The *monopoly* theory of international trade is logical and explains some trade, but a small, decreasing fraction. This is that every producer wants to be a price-discriminating monopolist and that the easiest way to become one is to export. Geographical segregation of markets is relatively simple in this case and different prices can be set at home and abroad, or even in each export market, so as to equate marginal revenue and marginal cost in each market. Price discrimination is rife, whisky is priced at about 30 per cent of its European level in Britain, cars at almost twice the level (in both cases net of tax and retail margins). However, whilst exporting provides opportunities for price discrimination, the latter may not be the motive for it.

The *economies of scale* theory is logical but empirically irrelevant. This argues that if there were economies of scale, identical countries could gain by specialisation. This is true. (Take two countries; either could produce 30x, 30y or 10 of each. Assume x and y are perfect complements, without trade each produces 10 of x and 10 of y. If either of them specialises in x and the other in y each will consume 15x and 15y.) However, there is no evidence that economies of scale exist such that national economies are too small to exploit them and much evidence that trade patterns are inconsistent with such a theory.

The '*vent for surplus*' theory is associated with Williams and Myint. In essence, their proposition is that many underdeveloped economies are inside their production possibility frontiers and that the stimulus of trade is necessary to ensure the full utilisation of resources. The argument would certainly have met with the approval of colonial governors in British Africa who deliberately sought to promote both internal and external trade for this reason. However, it is probably more relevant to a theory of development than of trade. Trade more often occurs because it is profitable than because of a belief that it is essential for development. Even in the colonial case, the actual trade was carried out by British (and Asian) entrepreneurs. In post-colonial Africa, governments have usually sought to restrict trade, not promote it.

The simplest of the *political* theories is that trade is an arm of diplomacy. Nations trade so as to encourage better relations. Often trade ties are imposed by the stronger as a means of making the weaker into a dependency. This theory reverses the economic theory of imperialism, whereby power was sought to promote trade ('trade follows the flag'). Instead, trade, even unprofitable trade, is sought as a means to power. Examples are legion: perhaps the most blatant being Franco-German competition in Eastern Europe between the wars.

Marxism argues that trade occurs as an essential stage in the self-destructive progress of capitalism towards its inevitable doom. Firms seek profits abroad as they decline at home but, of course, this merely intensifies the competition, as the same is happening in every country. Such ideas are hard to present in a way that is neither a caricature nor misleading but are nevertheless capable of penetrating insights, e.g. Glyn and Sutcliffe (1972).

2.10 The Pure Theory in the Real World

The acid test of the pure theory is to see if it can explain the patterns of trade that actually exist. Problems arise because many countries' exports and imports are remarkably similar, e.g. Britain both exports and imports cars on a large scale. France and Germany each exports large numbers of cars to the other. Britain both exports and imports high-technology capital-intensive goods like computers and has a similar two-way trade in low-technology labour-intensive shirts.

The factor endowment theory, while very successful at explaining the internal organisation of Ford or ITT, cannot explain such behaviour. There is no way in which it can be argued that French cars are more or less labour-intensive than German ones.

The Ricardian theory does somewhat better. It sometimes uses the rather formalistic device of saying that each make of car is a separate good and comparative advantage exists in them. Italy has a comparative advantage in making Italian cars, indeed no one else can make an Italian car. This is reasonable for a few goods — Paris fashions, British shotguns

— but is not generally very acceptable. More convincing use is made of Lancaster's 'characteristics' theory. This argues that all goods are bundles of 'primary characteristics'. Thus, a car is a bundle of, *inter alia*, performance, comfort, economy and style. It is then argued that different countries have comparative advantage in these characteristics but no one can buy a characteristic without a car. Hence Italian style or German reliability or Japanese gadgets have to be embodied in superficially similar cars. The problem with comparative advantage may be that it is so flexible that it could explain anything.

Appendix: Factor Reversals

The concept of factor reversals is best understood by reference to a diagram such as Figure 2.2 which has the capital:labour ratio on the horizontal axis and the relative cost of capital in terms of labour on the vertical axis. The optimal capital: labour ratio for each level of (relative) costs is then plotted as in Figure 2.2(a). If there are fixed proportions of factors in production this curve would be vertical, but normally it would slope downwards from left to right as in Figure 2.2(a). As the cost of capital falls relative to wages, it becomes profitable to substitute capital for labour so the capital:labour ratio rises. If one plots these curves for two industries on the same diagram it is possible to see whether a reversal of factor intensity occurs. If the curves intersect, as in Figure 2.2(b), a reversal occurs. x represents the optimal capital output ratio for industry X and y for industry Y. At relative cost level c_1 industry Y has a higher capital:labour ratio; r_1 compared to r_2. As the relative cost of capital falls there is a reversal of factor intensity such that at relative cost level c_2 industry X is more capital intensive since its capital:labour ratio (r_3) is higher than Y's (r_4). Where the curves do not intersect there is no reversal. For the FPET it is necessary only that there be no reversal over the relevant range, i.e. between the initial relative cost (factor payments) in the two countries. Hence the case illustrated in Figure 2.2(c) satisfies this requirement, even though a reversal would occur at an irrelevant ratio. The problem of factor reversals was extensively analysed by Minhas (reprinted in Bhagwati, 1969, pp. 140-68). Minhas argued that such reversals were important empirically as well as theoretically.

Figure 2.2: Factor Reversals

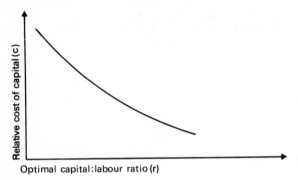

a) The relationship between relative cost and the optimal ratio

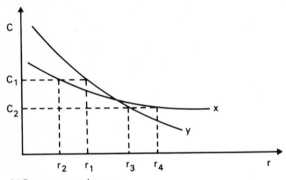

b) Factor reversal occurs

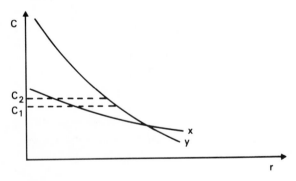

c) Irrelevant factor reversal

c_1 is initial cost ratio in Country 1 and c_2 in Country 2. Trade would equalise factor prices.

Note

1. The FPET can be demonstrated geometrically, e.g. Grubel (1977), pp. 48-52 and 54-8, and Johnson (1958), Chapter 1, which also discussed the case where factor intensities are reversed. An algebraic proof can be found in Batra (1973), p. 117.

3 COMMERCIAL POLICY I: TARIFFS AND THE THEORY OF PROTECTION

3.1 Some Concepts

Free trade exists if imports are allowed to compete on equal terms with domestic suppliers without any device introduced by governments to try to distort the choice of purchasers. Domestic producers may very well enjoy some *natural protection*, because of transport costs (or, in the extreme, geography). For example, a restaurant in Singapore cannot compete on equal terms for my custom with one in York. A painter in Germany could tender to paint York University, but his travelling costs handicap him such that he cannot be said to compete on level terms with York painters. Economists recognise this but normally simplify their analysis to consideration of only two types of goods:

1. *traded goods* in which free trade could exist if governments permitted it, i.e. there are no transport costs, and
2. *non-traded goods* in which there could never be any foreign competition, let alone free trade, i.e. transport costs are prohibitive.

This distinction is used in various places in the subsequent analysis, e.g. Chapter 10. Before leaving natural protection, it is worth noting that it may protect the importer against the domestic producer. A Californian firm, for example, has much lower transaction costs in reaching Vancouver than a firm in Quebec.

Protection exists when imports are handicapped in their ability to compete with domestic goods. By convention, 'protection' is restricted to those cases where governments have imposed the handicap, i.e. natural protection is excluded. There are many protective devices.

3.1.1 Tariffs

A tariff is a tax which is imposed on imports but not on domestically produced goods. The tax may be a flat rate or *specific* one – e.g. £500 per car. Alternatively, tariffs may be calculated as a percentage of the importers' price, an *ad valorem* tariff, e.g. 20 per cent. Tariffs can be calculated in other ways – e.g. the US government used to calculate them as a percentage of the domestic producers' price, the American selling price system. Often it is debatable whether a tariff has been imposed or not, since it is not clear whether the same tax is paid on imported goods as on domestically produced ones. This may seem strange, but stems from ambiguity about the definition of a good. Wine is imported into the UK and pays a high rate of tax (for the purposes of this argument the miniscule UK production is ignored). Bitter beer is produced domestically and pays a much lower rate of tax. This arrangement might be argued to be protective since imported alcohol pays a higher rate of tax than domestically produced alcohol; an argument advanced by the European Commission in 1981 and Gladstone in 1860 amongst others. Alternatively if wine and beer are separate products there is no tariff.

A tariff which is sufficiently high to exclude all imports is called a *prohibitive tariff.*

3.1.2 Quotas

A quota restricts the amount, either by value or volume, of a product which can be imported. Quotas, for example, are imposed by most OECD countries on textile imports, either through multilateral arrangements like the MFA (Multilateral Fibre Arrangement) or unilaterally. Quotas take various forms depending upon the arrangements made to determine who is allowed to supply the restricted quantity.

3.1.3. Subsidies

A subsidy may be used to induce domestic residents not to buy imports e.g. at the time of writing the UK government is to give £10 million ... made it to have a replacement for the *Atlantic Conveyor* ... astle rather than South Korea. Subsidies may be ... ded to all purchasers, or specific to the individual ... ase. They may be paid to consumers or producers ... ne.

... permitted by GATT (p. 29 above). An import ... nporter to lodge, usually with the central bank, a ... ne cost of the import interest free for a period of ... nths or one year. Import deposits were used by the ... in 1976. In both cases it seems to have been very ... ecause of the macroeconomic effects of the forced ... at than because of any protective effect.

3.1.5 State Trading Monopolies

These are probably the oldest and most widespread of protective devices, being used in Ancient Egypt and in virtually every country in the communist bloc, Africa, Asia and Latin America. The government permits no one but itself to import a named good. It then resells the good to domestic consumers, usually at a profit. Alternatively, the right may be delegated to a specific person or company — usually for a cash payment. Elizabeth I made extensive use of such trading monopolies but renounced them in 1601 after the 'Golden Speech'. They were just as controversial in the UK after World War II when used by the Labour government, although reducing substantially the cost of imports (Ady's analysis: pp. 553-9 of Worswick and Ady, 1952) but being selected by the Conservatives as one of the major oppressive devices from which they would 'set the people free' — the Conservative slogan in the 1950 election.

3.1.6 Non-tariff Barriers to Trade

Logically, a non-tariff barrier would include (1) to (5) but is usually, although not always, restricted to a barrage of administrative and regulatory devices which restrict trade. These range from preferential buying to sophisticated restrictions masquerading as health and safety regulations. Preferential buying occurs when public sector bodies buy more expensive domestic goods in preference to cheaper imports. This is enshrined in the 'Buy American' Acts (which lay down a percentage by which an import must undercut the domestic price before it is purchased) and was practised in the 1960s and 1970s by the UK government in its computer policy to help ICL against IBM. Even here the line is blurred, as protection may take the form of specifying a feature that only the domestic product could have, even though not intrinsically desirable; this is especially common in defence purchases (Hartley (1983).

The regulatory and administrative devices used to restrict trade are legion but are impossible to distinguish from genuine safety and health regulations. For example, German brewers have always used a method of production which does not use the additives used by British, Belgian and Dutch producers. Is a regulation banning the sale of beer with additives in Germany discriminatory? The Germans argue that the additives are dangerous to health; the EEC Commission that it is a protective ploy. European producers of cars have argued that US safety and pollution regulations impose, and were intended to impose, a cost penalty on them compared to US producers. American producers deny this, with justice, but the Japanese government recently amended its regulations because it agreed that they had an (unintentional?) protective effect.

3.2 The Effective Rate of Protection

It is important, given the array of protective devices, that a measure of protection be available. The standard measure is the effective rate of protection. This is calculated so that as far as possible protection can be analysed as if there were a tariff on a good with no inputs, i.e. the simplest possible microeconomic problem. The calculations assume that incidence is always on the consumer; this follows from the 'small country' assumption below but would also follow from an assumption of perfectly inelastic demand, a common assumption in tax analysis. In this case any tariff will be added to the world price of the good and any subsidy will be retained by the producer.

The first problems which arise in calculating protection arise from the existence of inputs. Tariffs on these affect the competitive position of domestic firms, e.g. a tariff on wheat clearly affects the ability of flour-millers to compete on equal terms with foreigners. The ERP in this case is:

$$ERP = \frac{\text{Tariff on Output} - \text{Tariff on input}}{\text{Value Added of Industry } \textit{measured at world prices}}$$

To take a specific example. If at world prices (i.e. free trade prices) it requires £40 worth of iron ore to make £100 worth of steel, the ERP will be calculated for a 20 per cent tariff on steel and a 12½ per cent tariff on iron ore, as:

$$ERP = \frac{\text{Tariff on output (20 per cent of 100)} - \text{Tariff on input (12½ per cent of 40)}}{\text{Value added (100-40)}}$$

$$= \frac{20-5}{60}$$

$$= \frac{15}{60} = 25 \text{ per cent}$$

The rationale is that protection should be calculated as a percentage of value added, i.e. the industry's net output, so the £20 tariff (20 per cent of gross output) is equal to protection of one-third on net output. On the other hand, the firm has to pay £45 for its inputs instead of a free trade price of £40, so this extra cost acts as negative protection and needs to be deducted from the £20 tariff.

If there is a tariff on an input into an input, this is similarly calculated — does it affect the price the firm pays? Thus if instead of the iron ore tariff there were a coal tariff, it would have no effect on the price of iron ore and so no effect on the ERP of steel.

Subsidies can be added to the ERP. A subsidy of £15 per unit of steel (i.e. £100 worth of final output at world prices) adds 25 per cent to the ERP, i.e. 15 divided by the value added at world prices. Subsidies on inputs, however have no effect on the ERP being retained by the producers of the inputs. All other protective devices are similarly converted into cost penalties for foreign producers or cost bonuses for domestic producers. In the case of quotas this requires additional assumptions and is discussed below in the context of comparing tariffs and quotas.

The only remaining point about the ERP is to note that it is often negative (e.g. Oulton, 1976). If the tariff on the input is sufficiently high, this can happen even when the nominal tariff is very high. In the above example if the steel tariff were 100 per cent and the iron ore tariff 300 per cent the ERP would be:

$$\text{ERP} = \frac{100 - 120}{60} = -33\,^1/_3 \text{ per cent.}$$

Another quirk arises when the value added at world prices is negative; in this case the ERP is infinite by definition. This is true of some Northumberland hill farmers. However, it is perhaps simpler to take the (fictitious) case of growing tomatoes in Greenland. It would require about £600 worth of oil to heat greenhouses that would produce tomatoes that could be bought in Holland for £100. The total cost of inputs might be £800. In this case the industry's value added would be -£700. However a 900 per cent tariff on tomatoes would raise the price in Greenland to £1000 and make it profitable to produce them there. (The cost figures are approximately accurate, the tariff is fictitious.)

3.3 The Case for Free Trade

Anglo-Saxon economists have traditionally been advocates of free trade, unlike their continental European *confrères* who have usually been protectionist. Sometimes advocates of free trade have been so hysterical that it obscures the respectable and soundly based tradition of protectionist argument. For example, Hirst (1911) wrote:

> If those who made the war had been allowed to make a tariff, the greatest shipping broking and banking centre of the world would have been not only shaken but shattered. *Grass would have grown in the port of London and in the streets of the City.* (p. 72)

Samuelson's standard text states:

> 'No fair-minded reader who takes the trouble to think the matter through can fail to see how shallow are most of the economic arguments for tariff protection. The only obvious exception is the infant-industry argument. (p. 703, 10th edition)

Even this passage is less strident than the equivalent in earlier editions. It is therefore worthy of note that the US, Germany and Japan all became great economic powers when pursuing highly protectionist policies, and some argue their success was because of protection.

The original case for free trade was a natural extension of the argument in Chapter 2. Once international trade was shown to be beneficial, any restriction was taken to be undesirable. A more modern version of the argument uses the paretian welfare argument for a competitive economy. (There is no difference between the argument for permitting domestic trade and for foreign trade.) Any restriction on trade will produce a distortion that interferes with one or other paretian criteria. Figure 3.1 shows this argument, in the diagram used in the previous chapter. The production possibility frontier is PF, the consumption possibility frontier CD. If there is free trade, market forces will operate such that consumers equate the marginal rate of substitution with the world price, so consumption will be at X, where the indifference curve is tangential. Protection is designed to distort choice, through an alteration of price or otherwise, to reduce imports and increase the consumption of domestic goods. If world prices are unchanged, consumers will finish up at some point with consumption of x between the autarkic point A and X, shown as Y on Figure 3.1. Y is, by definition, on a lower indifference curve than X and so inferior to it. Free trade is a potential pareto gain compared to protection but it will only be an *actual* pareto gain if there is:

Figure 3.1: The Effects of Protection

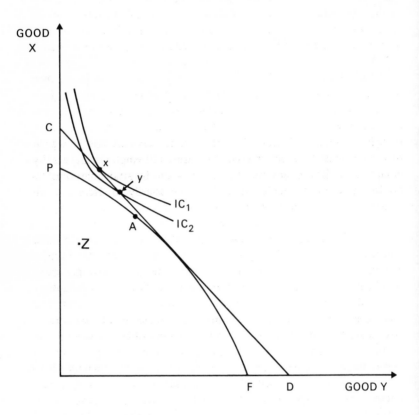

1. full employment;
2. indifference to the distribution of income (or lump sum transfers to ensure an optimal distribution);

In addition the argument implicitly assumed:

3. fixed world prices;
4. a static economy.

The major protectionist arguments depend upon a relaxation of any of these assumptions.

3.4 The Case for Protection

The major economic arguments for protection stem from a relaxation of the assumptions necessary to show the optimality of free trade. In most cases there is a free trade counter-argument which reveals that protection would be the best attainable state rather than an ideal state.

3.4.1 Unemployment

If an economy would otherwise have unemployment, there may be a case for protection. In Figure 3.1, if the economy were at point Z, then protection would be desirable if it moved the economy to Y (even though X would be better still). The free traders have always argued that there must be a better way of ensuring full employment, e.g. by monetary or fiscal policy (in this case X would be attainable). Protectionists have always denied that this is necessarily so. Here the full employment case for protection will be analysed in two forms, the macroeconomic and microeconomic one.

The macroeconomic argument is either the Keynesian foreign trade multiplier or a monetarist argument that a balance of payments surplus will increase the money supply and so income. This latter argument goes back to Mun and the other mercantilists derided by protectionists since Adam Smith. The argument is, however, perfectly valid. The only question is, can economic expansionism be secured by more ortho-dox means? In some cases it argued this as impossible. It might be that all the excess demand would be spent on imports. Alternatively the excess demand would produce a balance of payments deficit which was unacceptable or unsustainable. The balance of payments is con-sidered below in Chapters 6 to 8 and 10. However, as the macro-protectionist argument is now the major one used by advocates of import restrictions, it cannot be ignored in this context. The UK Labour Party's 'Alternative Economic Strategy' is entirely based upon this (see p. 99 below). Keynes, otherwise a life-long free trader, endorsed this protectionist argument in 1930 (Keynes (1930)).[1]

One problem with the macroeconomic argument for protection is that it represents an attempt to export unemploynent, unless the 'paradox of imports' (p. 103 below) applies. However, protectionists are rarely concerned with the welfare of other nations. Even an ultra-nationalist must take note of the danger of retaliation, which may simply lead to a reduction of employment and trade in all countries — the vicious cycle of 'beggar-my-neighbour' policies allegedly seen between the wars. (The importance of it depends upon how instrumental the US Smoot-Hawley tariff of 1930 was in triggering the European slump.)

The microeconomic employment case for protection starts with the obvious point that a tariff can increase the demand for labour in a specific place or industry. A tariff on steel in the US would raise employment in Pennsylvania. This is only relevant if there is no better way of raising Pennsylvanian employment. Effectively this is so if the shadow wage, or opportunity cost of labour, is less than the market price. This may be so. To take a much cited example, shipbuilding in the UK. Most shipbuilding workers are over 50 years of age and have no other job opportunities; they live in depressed areas and retraining or moves to the south-east are ruled out as too expensive (economically or socially). In this case their opportunity cost is low, possibly zero. Hence protection which led to their being employed would almost certainly improve resource allocation.

There are two free trade counters to this:

1. The general point that a subsidy would be preferable to a tariff – although this is still protection. If the opportunity cost of a Newcastle boilermaker is £20 and the wage rate £100, then a subsidy of £80 to the employer is optimal. This is true in principle; the point is discussed in the comparison of tariffs and subsidies, section 7 below.
2. Moreover, this argument is very easy to misapply and, like most citations of market failure, opens a Pandora's box of dangers. Virtually anyone can use a variant of this shadow price argument to justify protection. This is true but the theoretical argument remains.

3.4.2 The Distribution of Income

Tariffs will normally increase the income of those who produce the protected good and almost invariably increase their relative income. This desire to change the distribution of income is probably the main reason for the imposition of tariffs, at least in Australia and the US. Moreover, this is the main rationale of the CAP, i.e. a desire to increase the economic welfare of farmers albeit at the cost of others. In terms of Figure 3.1, X may be pareto preferred to Y, but the distribution of income at Y may be less socially desirable than at X. The extreme paretian would argue for a lump-sum redistribution of income and the maintenance of free trade (for a definition and discussion of 'lump-sum' transfers see p. 49 below). However, lump-sum transfers may be impossible or politically infeasible. In this case redistribution by protection may be the best available policy.

3.4.3 World Prices and the Terms of Trade

The free trade case assumes that a nation is unable to influence world prices, i.e. that the terms of trade are exogenous. It may be that by reducing the quantity it imports, a nation can reduce its input prices and so make itself better off. (This argument is also analysed on pp. 43ff below.) This is illustrated in Figure 3.2. The protectionist policy lowers the price of imports in terms of exports and so allows a new consumption possibility frontier, at least over a limited range. It may be that producing at P_2 and consuming at W is better than P_1 and X_1 respectively. In an extreme case it may be that consumption of both goods rises, if the increase in domestic production exceeds the fall in imports (imports must fall, otherwise there is no possibility of the terms of trade improving).

A tariff which ensures the maximum welfare gain from changing the terms of trade is called an 'optimum tariff'. This does not mean the tariff which produces the most favourable terms of trade − the gain caused by an improvement is after a point offset by the loss in consumers' surplus caused by lower consumption of the good. The optimum tariff allows for 'optimum retaliation', that is other countries will retaliate if it pays them to but not out of spite. The optimal tariff with retaliation is unlikely to be the same as without.

No protectionist argument has been so deeply analysed as the terms of trade one. It is not without relevance to the real world. The UK's import policy used to have a significant effect on the price of most raw materials and US policy still does. Classic examples are UK imports of New Zealand lamb and US purchases of coffee. The EEC has a major impact on world food prices. Nevertheless, in practice the terms of trade agreement would rarely seem to be relevant to the debate about protection.

3.4.4 Dynamic Arguments

The analysis used to justify free trade assumes that production possibility frontiers are fixed. It may be that if production of one good were increased, then 'learning economies' or some other dynamic factor would shift the production possibility frontier outwards over time. The benefits of this, appropriately discounted, could outweigh the short-term costs of protection. This is called the infant-industry or young economy agrement. Free traders counter argue that a subsidy might be

Figure 3.2: Terms of Trade Gain

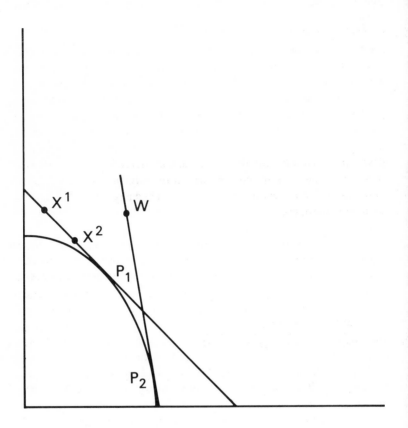

Extreme case: original consumption is X_2 and final consumption is at W so consumption of both goods has risen.

preferable or that tariffs may induce continued inefficiency. The longer-term effects of tariffs are very contentious. Tariffs may provide a secure shelter that permits long-run development, as in nineteenth-century Germany. They may protect an outdated, inefficient and complacent industrial structure, as in France until World War II.

3.4.5 Other Protectionist Arguments

There are a variety of other protectionist arguments that merit brief examination:

Countervailing Power. This is an argument that tariffs are necessary as bargaining counters in tariff negotiations. In other words, a classic deterrence argument with the usual problems this entails.

Non-economic Goals. The title for this category of arguments is misplaced since all of them amount to a statement that an industry's existence or output render an externality not captured in market prices, but the usual tag will be used. It is argued that certain industries are desirable because they render an economy or nation less dependent on others — usually used for defence-related industries, e.g. steel or shipbuilding, but often extended to cover a wide range of output especially in the field of energy. 'A gentleman needs a necktie, a nation an airline,' as a cynical American put it. A more sophisticated variation of this is to reduce foreign trade as a percentage of income to make a nation less susceptible to the world trade cycle — or less dependent on the income from a single export. A related set of arguments concern the desirability of trading with one group of nations rather than another either to show hostility to the latter or to foster friendship with the former. The counter agreements are the usual 'subsidy' or 'slippery slope' propositions. The latter has some force, given the range of industries which European governments seem to feel essential to national pride, ranging from computers to banking via aircraft production and soft drinks (the French government felt dependence on Coca-Cola derogatory to French culture).

Revenue. This argument is that all taxes distort but some tax is necessary so a tariff may be less objectionable than alternatives.

Dumping. This is a complex argument that if a foreign country subsidises its exports ('dumping'), it is right to impose a tariff. This was used to justify Britain's first modern peacetime departure from free trade in November 1919. It became very controversial in 1982 because the US government threatened to impose 'anti-dumping' duties on European steel — the subsidy in most cases is that the state owns the industry and permits enormous losses.

The argument often seems to be as much ethical as economic — *unfair* competition is wrong rather than harmful. Dumping *per se* is not undesirable for the importing country; e.g. arguably France has 'dumped' champagne in the UK, or did until the UK joined the EEC. No one could argue that the UK would have gained from a higher champagne price. The extreme free trader would argue that one should snap up cheap imports and use domestic labour to produce something else, but this is usually impracticable. Hence the pros and cons of dumping are hard to assess. The short-run opportunity cost of domestic production is often very low when faced with subsidised imports, especially in a recession. In this case the economic case for an anti-dumping duty is established; otherwise the argument is ethical not economic.

Note

1. Keynes marked his conversion by citing his early classic statement of the free trade position:

It will be fairest, perhaps, to quote, as an example, what I wrote myself. So lately as 1923, as a faithful pupil of the classical school who did not at that time doubt what he had been taught and entertained on this matter no reserves at all, I wrote: 'If there is one thing that protection can *not* do, it is to cure Unemployment . . . There are some arguments for Protection, based upon its securing possible but improbable advantages, to which there is no simple answer. But the claim to cure Unemployment involves the Protectionist fallacy in its grossest and crudest form.'

4 COMMERCIAL POLICY II: THE EFFECTS OF PROTECTION

4.1 The Effects of Tariffs

The effects of the imposition of a tariff on a particular good are best examined within the framework of the 'tariff triangle' diagram, Figure 4.1. This diagram in its simplest form requires a number of assumptions, which will be relaxed later.

1. the home market would otherwise be perfectly competitive, or at least have price takers on both sides;
2. the market for the good always clears by price; often omitted, this is necessary for any partial equilibrium comparative static analysis — including all supply and demand analysis.
3. the economy is a small one, i.e. no action by the country can influence world prices.

In Figure 4.1, HS is the home supply curve, as always this is also the industry's marginal cost curve. D is the home demand curve for the product (assumption (1) is required to permit these curves to be drawn). As the economy is a small one, it faces a perfectly elastic supply curve at the world price (WP). Foreign suppliers are prepared to offer unlimited quantities for sale at this price but will never charge less. Hence, with free trade, domestic producers must charge WP — any more and they sell nothing; any less and they are irrationally sacrificing profit to no purpose. Consequently the intersection of the perfectly elastic world supply curve (WP) with the (home) demand curve determines home consumption, Q_{CF} and with the home supply curve, domestic production, Q_{PF}. Imports are the difference between these, i.e. $Q_{CF} - Q_{PF}$.

Having established the free trade equilibrium, it is now possible to compare it with the equilibrium after the introduction of a tariff, either *ad valorem* or specific. The tariff raises the domestic price by the full amount of the tariff because the supply curve is still perfectly elastic but at (WP + T) where T is the tariff. Domestic producers are irrational to charge less than (WP + T) but unable to charge more than this because of the unlimited quantities being offered at this price, i.e. the foreign supply price plus the tariff. In fact the purchasers and suppliers

Figure 4.1: The Effects of a Tariff

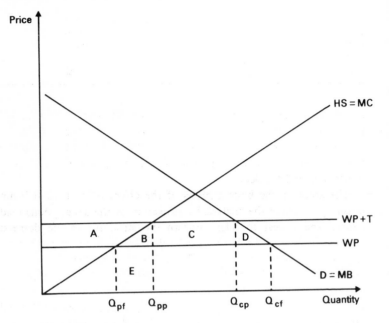

are in exactly the same position as before except that the price is higher. Domestic output rises from Q_{PF} to Q_{PP}, i.e. there is a move along the home supply curve. The higher price reduces (domestic) demand to Q_{CP}. Imports are, therefore, $Q_{CP} - Q_{PP}$.

It is now possible to establish the welfare effects of a tariff by the familiar 'area analysis' or surplus analysis using Figure 4.1. The calculation is set out in Table 4.1. Consumers' surplus falls by (A+B+C+D) because of the higher price. Producers' profits rise by A — their revenue rises by (A+B+E) but their costs rise by (B+E); the total cost is the area under the marginal cost curve, hence the cost of producing $(Q_{PP}-Q_{PF})$ is B+E. The tariff revenue accruing to the government is C; imports times tariff. Thus a tariff lowers community welfare by (B+D) and transfers A from consumers to producers and C from consumers to the government. The social cost (B+D) is a representation of the case for the potential pareto superiority of free trade. However, the income redistribution might well represent the objective of the tariff.

The two areas of social loss 'B' and 'D' are usually referred to as the 'production effect' and 'consumption effect' respectively. B is called the production effect because it is the excess of the cost of

Table 4.1: The Effect of a Tariff

	Gain (+)	Loss (-)
Consumers		– A – B – C – D
Government	+C	
Producers	+A	
Society		– B – D

domestic production (B+E) compared to foreign production (E); implicitly this assumes the world price equals the marginal cost of production. 'D' is the 'consumption effect', because it is that portion of the reduction in consumers' surplus caused by lower consumption rather than higher price.

The above is the basic analysis of the effect of a tariff. It is now possible to extend the analysis by relaxation of the assumptions made above. The easiest to relax concern the structure of the domestic market. So long as the tariff is not prohibitive, even a sole purchaser or supplier has no market power. This analysis is developed further, p. 50 below, where tariffs are compared with quotas which can create monopoly. Hence only minor modifications are necessary to Figure 4.1 to show the cases of a sole domestic purchaser or supplier. The sole domestic purchaser in fact merely requires the relabelling of the demand curve as the marginal benefit curve; there is no demand curve with a monopsonist. The demand curve is always the MB curve anyway so this generalisation affects none of the analysis. The sole domestic supplier is equally simple. There is no longer a supply curve, merely a marginal cost curve. WP and (WP+T) represent the suppliers' marginal revenue curve – so long as the tariff is non-prohibitive. Hence, for a non-prohibitive tariff all the above analysis still holds. A prohibitive tariff reduces the analysis to the elementary microeconomic supply and demand diagrams and the normal comparison of competition and mono-monopsony or monopoly can be made. With a prohibitive tariff, there are no imports and so no tariff revenue.

The terms of trade case is more interesting and is illustrated in Figure 4.2. The crucial difference is that the world supply curve is upward sloping at WS. To simplify the diagram, the HS and D curves have been replaced by a single excess demand or demand for imports (DM) curve. This is equal to home demand less home supply. It is obviously more elastic than either HS or D since it shows the *sum* of the responses of supply and demand to a change in price. A change in the 'consumers' surplus triangle' represents the net change in both consumers' surplus and profits, i.e. (B+C+D) in Figure 4.1. Under free trade

Figure 4.2: A Tariff Improves the Terms of Trade

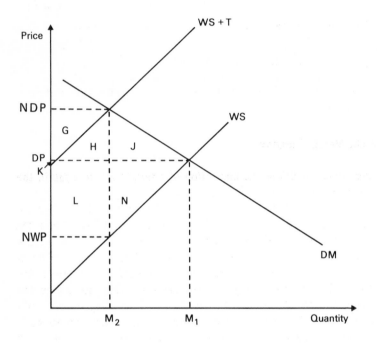

the demand for imports is M_1 and both world and domestic price are equal to DP. The tariff shifts the supply curve by T, upwards to (WS+T) (here T is specific) so the domestic price rises to NDP and imports fall to M_2. The new world price is NWP; the analysis is, of course, the most elementary of tax analyses, as in Lipsey (1979), Chapter 11.

The welfare analysis, set out in Table 4.2, is that consumers and producers together lose (G+H+J). The tariff revenue is (G+H+K+L), M_2 times T. Hence the net welfare gain is (K+L) − J. Thus there may be a net gain to the country improving the tariff by improving its terms of trade. World suppliers lose (K+L+N) so the tariff imposes a cost on the world as a whole of (J+N), the Marshallian triangle. This analysis has therefore confirmed that, on p. 33 above, a tariff must reduce world welfare but may benefit the country imposing it.

Table 4.2: Welfare Gains and Losses of a Tariff Which Improves the Terms of Trade

	Gain (+)	Loss (−)
Producers and Consumers	− (G − H − J)	
Government	+ G + H + K + L	
Country imposing tariff	− J + (K + L)	
Producers in the rest of the world	− K − L − N	
World	− J − N	

4.2 The Metzler Paradox

Under some conditions the imposition of a tariff leads to a *fall* in the domestic price of the good. In other words, foreign suppliers reduce their price by more than the amount of the tariff. This is called the Metzler paradox (Metzler, 1949). This arises because of the effect of the tariff on the income of the foreign producers. This decrease in income reduces their consumption of their own good such that there is a shift in the world supply curve. Examples are rare; Ghanaian cocoa in the 1960s and New Zealand lamb being the most plausible. This case is shown in Figure 4.3 when the new equilibrium is reached; the diagram is a modified version of Figure 4.2. The WS curve has shifted from WS to WS^N. The consequence is that the domestic price *falls* from DP to NDP and the world price from DP to NWP. Imports rise from M_1 to M_2. Consumers and producers together gain (A+B+C); actually of course consumers gain more than this and producers lose. The tariff revenue is (D+E+F+G+H) so the overall effect is highly favourable to the tariff-improving country.

The effect only arises if:

1. the country is large;
2. the exporting countries consume large enough quantities of the good to generate an income effect on the world supply curve;
3. the income effect is large enough to offset the effect of the tariff.

These conditions will only be met when the elasticity of the world supply curve is sufficiently low and the propensity of the exporters to consume the good is sufficiently high; the formal conditions necessarily involve an elasticity of less than one. The paradox is rare and is more useful in highlighting the 'income effect' which is likely to arise for many raw materials, although not enough to offset the size of a tariff. Such effects have also been generated by the CAP; Third World producers of food and New Zealand being those whose income has suffered.

Figure 4.3: The Metzler Paradox

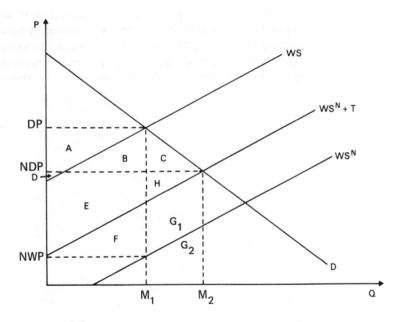

4.3 Tariffs and the Income of Producers

It was argued above that one of the major objectives of protection was to enrich those who produce the protected good. This effect was clearly shown in section 3.5. However, there are circumstances in which the imposition of a tariff actually lowers the income of those producing the good. Two of these have been mentioned *en passant*.

4.3.1 If the ERP Is Negative

This is arguably a theoretically trivial but practically relevant consideration. A tariff, or other protection, is often introduced as part of a whole
schedule of tariffs so an industry may suffer negative protection. UK
beef farmers have argued that the CAP works in this fashion since its
effects in raising the price of cattle food outweigh the apparent protection. This 'danger' was always in the front of the minds of those design-
ing US tariffs especially the McKinley tariff (1890) and Dingley tariff
(1897). They devoted painstaking care to ensure that no producer lost
out as a result of a Tariff Act or at least no producer interest associated
with the Republican Party.

4.3.2 When the Metzler Paradox Applies

Obviously if a tariff lowers the domestic price, the domestic producers
will lose revenue.

Barring these cases, the argument concerns what is usually called the
Stolper-Samuelson Theorem (1941): that protection will raise the real
income of the factor(s) used intensively in producing the protected
good. The theory is usually presented in a two-good, two-factor model
in which the result concerns the effect on real wages of protecting a
labour-intensive industry. It is much more relevant to consider the
theorem in an 'n factor' world in which the intensive factors are those
specific to an industry. Protection of textiles would, when the theorem
held, raise the income of both textile industry shareholders and workers
skilled in crafts specific to the textile industry. However, on simple
assumptions, it would not affect, or would even reduce, the incomes of
either unskilled workers or workers with general skills (e.g. typists)
employed in the industry.

Their employment might rise but the effect on the demand for
general labour would be so small that wages would not rise. In practice,
given labour immobility and the geographical concentration of
industry, protection would probably raise the wages of all workers.

The partial analysis in section 4.1 seemed to show that tariffs would
raise the income of the producer, so it may seem that Stopler-
Samuelson is self-evident. In fact, the 'general equilibrium' factors
which may affect the validity theorem stem from the fact that those
producing the good may lose as consumers. *If the producers do not
consume their own good, the theorem is necessarily valid.*

Moreover *a tariff must raise both the money income and the share
of national income going to the producers.* However as prices are
higher, and national income lower, this does not establish that their

real incomes are higher. In measuring *real* incomes there is, as usual, an index number problem because the tariff changes relative prices. It can be shown that *producer incomes rise when measured at free trade prices* but not necessarily at the new prices. Bhagwati (1959) argues that the result in this case depends upon:

1. whether tariffs are prohibitive (*prohibitive tariffs necessarily raise producer income*);
2. income elasticies of demand (with unitary elasticities, the theorem is more likely to be upheld);
3. whether the elasticity of *foreign* demand for imports (EF) exceeds the domestic propensity to consume exportables (c) — *if EF > c, the theorem is necessarily true*;
4. the nature of production functions;
5. the precise definition of factor intensity;
6. whether factor intensities are reversible.

Altogether Bhagwati produces 14 cases by combining variants of these; in eight the effect of protection on producers' real incomes is indeterminate. Batra (1973) claims to show that an alternative sufficient condition is that the tariff on the output of an industry exceeds that on all its inputs. (This claim is not universally accepted.)

In conclusion it needs only to be said that protection will almost always raise producer real incomes; but the literature is a reminder that the apparently obvious should never be accepted without question.

4.4 Tariffs and Subsidies

The argument cited above that a subsidy always imposes lower welfare losses and so is preferable to a tariff is one example of the general paretian argument for subsidies as a means of achieving goals. In the case of tariffs, the free trader argues that one should ascertain the goal of protection and minimise the cost of achieving it. This will be by a subsidy rather than a tariff; free trade writers often regard a subsidy as non-protectionist although it is a different form of protection, even if theoretically it produces fewer distortions.

If the goal of protection is to raise producers' incomes, a cash transfer can achieve this without a welfare cost. Of course, the income effect of the subsidy may reduce the industry's output, but this does not matter so long as the goal is to raise the producers' overall standard of living. If a belief that hill farmers desire larger incomes is held, then if hill farmers choose to take the benefit as leisure rather than goods a subsidy's objective has still been achieved (at least on paretian criteria). If the objective is to raise the industry's output, e.g. for strategic reasons, a subsidy will avoid the 'consumption effect' but not the 'production effect'. This can be shown in Figure 4.1; instead of a tariff, a subsidy of T per unit would produce a parallel shift in the home supply curve such that output rose from Q_{PF} to Q_{PP}. Consumers are better off by (A+B+C+D) than with a tariff and the producers are in exactly the same position. The government pays a subsidy of (A+B) (i.e. T times Q_{PP}) instead of receiving a tax of C so it is worse off by (A+B+C). Hence a subsidy has a welfare gain of D compared to a tariff. (There is a loss of B, compared to free trade.) This demonstrates that a tariff is inferior to a subsidy as a means of stimulating output. The argument is generalisable to show that a subsidy is the minimum cost method of raising output.

Unfortunately there is a fatal flaw in the argument for subsidies, they have to be financed. The naive paretian argument assumes that they are financed by 'lump-sum' tax. A lump-sum tax is a tax that has no substitution effects although it may — probably would have — income effects. However, it is impossible to think of a practicable, let alone equitable, lump-sum tax. Taxes on potential earnings, Tinbergen's IQ tax and other schemes have been proposed but no one believes they are politially feasible and very few that they are practicable or just. To argue that the author of this book could have earned more writing romantic fiction instead and so he will be taxed on what he could have earned avoids any distortion of my choice about what to write. It is impossible to think of any other argument for it or any means of determining the maximum I could earn.

Hence subsidies have to be financed by taxes with distortionary effects or by inflation. In either case one must make a second-best comparison of the distortion caused by a subsidy and its associated tax with that caused by a tariff. The tariff may very well be the better means of increasing output or income transference. The whole debate is really one about political economy and some argue for subsidies because they are more overt and so more likely to arouse opposition and so less likely to be introduced or continued without good reason. Other arguments concern equity — if the EEC wishes to raise the income of Breton farmers, it is unfair and arbitrary to do it at the expense of butter consumers rather than of taxpayers generally.

4.5 Tariffs, Quotas and Competition

The effect of a tariff and a quota are relatively easy to compare using Figure 4.1. So long as the assumptions are valid, i.e. a small economy, markets clearing by price and atomistic markets, there will always be a tariff whose effects are equivalent to any quota.

A quota of $(Q_{CP} - Q_{PP})$ would have exactly the same effect as the tariff (T). If only this quantity of imports were available, price would rise to (WP+T), production rise to Q_{PP} and demand fall to Q_{CP} just as with the tariff. The only difference concerns area C, which is government (tariff) revenue in the tariff case. In the quota case it is a rent which accrues to the quota holder who is allowed to buy at WP and sell at (WP+T). This right may be auctioned by the government in which case it receives the revenue and there is no difference from the tariff case. It may be allocated to the foreign producer(s) who thereby acquire a valuable right. In fact it is possible for the foreign suppliers to do better out of protection than with free trade in this case. The right to sell a small quantity at a high price may very well be more profitable than competition which enables the sale of a large quantity at a low price. The most notorious (and much analysed) example of this is the US sugar quota. (The earliest analysis is Cater (1965), pp. 17-20 and pp. 199-204.) The right is more often parcelled out amongst domestic residents. In the US an almost unbelievable system of oil quotas provided their holders (the oil majors, Shell, BP, Exxon, etc.) with what was close to the proverbial licence to print money from 1953 to 1971. The restrictions on imports maintained the US price of oil well above world levels. A quota holder was permitted to purchase oil in the Middle East at $1.80 and resell at the US price of $3.45 (1971 figures). Both the US examples illustrate cases of the use of quota rents to buy off potential opposition to a protectionist policy. Quotas can finally be allocated to friends of the government – Elizabeth I practised this as well as the state trading monopoly. This is common in much of the Third World today and is often associated with various forms of corruption.

If the small country assumption is relaxed, big differences emerge between quotas and tariffs (Falvey, 1975)). For example, the Metzler paradox cannot occur with a quota. The terms of trade gain with a quota is in general less than with a tariff, although it depends upon how quotas are allocated and upon foreign market structures.

The most dramatic difference between tariffs and quotas occurs when there is a sole domestic producer. The analysis is illustrated in

Figure 4.4: Quotas and Monopoly

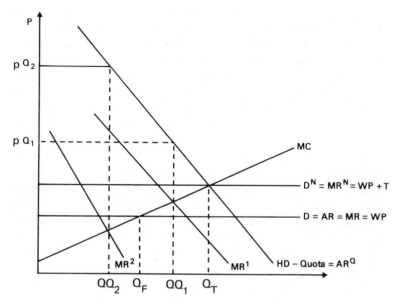

Figure 4.4. With free trade, the supplier is a price taker facing a horizontal marginal (and average) revenue curve at WP. Equilibrium output is, therefore, Q_F. A tariff has the effect of shifting the marginal revenue curve to (WP+T) but the supplier is still a price taker so MR is still equal to AR, the MR, and demand, curve is horizontal. Equilibrium output rises to Q_T (and price to WP+T). A quota, however, converts the latent market power of the sole supplier into actual monopoly power. At each price, the supplier will be able to sell (home demand − quota). This gives him a downward sloping demand curve. This demand curve (and AR curve) will pass through (Q_T, WP+T), i.e. the demand curve created by the quota whose effects would be equivalent to a tariff of T under perfect competition. At price (WP+T) the supplier can sell Q_T when imports are equal to the size of the quota. This is true whether imports are determined by a quota and price determined by the supplier or the price by the tariff and the quantity by the supplier. However, as the supplier is a price setter (monopolist), marginal revenue is no longer equal to average revenue. All that is known is that:

1. the derived demand curve (HD − quota) is more elastic than HD itself; the consequence of a leftward parallel shift of any demand

curve;

2. MR is less than AR.

The relevant marginal revenue curve could be either MR_1 or MR_2 in Figure 4.4.[1] In the MR_1 case output is Q_{Q1} and price P_{Q1}. Price is higher than in the tariff case and output lower but output is higher than in the free trade case. If MR_2 is the relevant marginal revenue curve, output will be Q_{Q2} and price P_{Q2} – i.e. output is less than the free trade case, as well as the tariff case.

In general the following are true:

1. A quota will lead to a price at least as high as with the equivalent tariff. The price will be higher unless the domestic industry is atomistic, and the economy is small.
2. A quota will lead to a domestic output no higher than the 'tariff equivalent' case. The output will be lower unless the domestic industry is atomistic and may even be less than with free trade.
3. A quota is certain to increase the income of producers and is almost certain to lead to a larger increase than for a tariff.

4.6 Tariffs and State Trading Monopolies

A state trading monopoly is capable of exploiting any terms of trade gain that might accrue to a nation; by restricting purchase they can reduce price if faced with an upward sloping supply curve. In fact it can act as a price discriminating monopsonist and so secure even greater gains than a tariff could; with a tariff all foreign suppliers receive the same price (see Gowland (1982(b)) for a discussion of price discriminating monopsony, pp. 183-4). State trading monopolies are usually used as a part of an overall *dirigiste* policy in which the allocation of imports is used as a key tool of planning and control. The monopoly may also seek to avoid a balance of payments problem by insisting on barter by paying for its imports directly with goods. The Nazi regime in Germany were experts at this tactic on occasion; e.g. insisting on discharging their import bill with aspirins (in 1939 they forced armaments on a surprised Yugoslavia). The communist states of Eastern Europe have copied the Nazis. The major exponents of state trading monopolies to improve the terms of trade were the post-war UK Labour government. In 1947, 1948 and 1949, 64, 61 and 58 per cent respectively of imports were state purchases (Ady's figures: Worswick and Ady (1954)). Because the purchases affected world prices, it is impossible, as Ady points out, to estimate the precise gain or compare it with the losses of consumers' surplus caused by lower consumption and less choice. The various special features of a state trading monopoly make it impossible to compare simply with tariffs, but in principle the effect would be exactly the same so long as the monopoly selected the quantity of world imports so as to maximise profits, so long as the atomistic assumption was valid and a uniform price was paid for imports. In many ways a state trading monopoly is similar to a quota, so that differences emerge in a world of uncertainty. A government commits itself to price with a tariff and to quantity with a quota but neither with a state trading monopoly. Hence the analysis presented above could not distinguish the three in the basic case where HS and D are taken as given. The theoretical case for state trading monopolies is impeccable, but both their antecedents and history justify extreme mistrust of their practical implementation. Profit maximisation is unlikely to be the goal of a state trading monopoly and corruption, favouritism or sheer inefficiency are likely to be prevalent even if worse sins are absent.

Note

1. For any demand curve, there can only be one marginal revenue curve of course but the demand curve could be such that either MR_1 or MR_2 is such. For completeness, the diagram should show alternative demand curves but this is not done to avoid rendering the diagram even harder to follow.

5 CUSTOMS UNIONS

5.1 Some Concepts

The best known of customs unions is the European Economic Community, or Common Market, founded by Germany, France, Italy and the Benelux countries in 1957 by the Treaty of Rome. In 1973 the UK, Denmark and Ireland joined, followed by Greece in 1981. Spain and Portugal are due to join by 1984 and Turkey may also join by 1990. Like its predecessor, the German Zollverein of the nineteenth century, the EEC has attempted to grow into something more than a customs union, but with much less success to date. The EEC has been copied without very much success by a variety of bodies in the Third World. However, before analysing customs unions, it is necessary to define them and some other superficially similar groupings of nations.

A *free trade area* is a group of nations who agree to remove all tariffs (and at least some other non-tariff barriers to trade) on trade amongst themselves. The best-known example is the European Free Trade Area, EFTA, founded under British auspices in 1958, which included, besides the UK, the Scandinavian countries and some other countries such as Portugal, Switzerland and Austria unable or unwilling to join the EEC. (Austria, for example, is constrained by treaty from membership of organisations like the EEC.)

If, in addition to forming a free trade area, the nations agree to impose a common external tariff, then a *customs union* has been formed. Its essential characteristic is therefore that its members agree on a common trading policy towards the rest of the world. Whereas, although both members of EFTA, the UK permitted unrestricted import of food but Denmark had a very protectionist policy until 1973, both had to adopt the same policy after they joined the EEC.

There are various types of customs unions but the differences are minor and mainly concern the division of the tariff revenue generated by the customs union. It may be spent centrally, as by the EEC, divided amongst the members according to a formula (the Zollverein) or kept by the country into which imports arrive. The latter is the most obvious but problems arise when imports destined for one member pass through another's territory; many of Gemany's imports enter the EEC through Antwerp. It would not be acceptable to Germany if the import duty on, say, sherry consumed by Germans were to be received by Belgium. Disputes over the allocation of customs revenue were one major factor in the break-up of the East African Customs Union (Tanzania, Kenya and Uganda) established in colonial times by the British.

There are three other types of economic association which usually involve even closer union than a customs union, although the concepts are less clearly defined. They are:

1. a *tax union*, in which the members agree on a common tax system;
2. an *economic union*, in which the members agree on common policies on such matters as regulation and, in some definitions, macroeconomic policy;
3. a *monetary union*, in which there is either a common currency or an unbreakable link between two or more currencies (Belgium and Luxemburg form a monetary union as the UK and Ireland did from 1921 to 1978).

5.2 Trade Diversion and Trade Creation

Customs unions have always induced something close to schizophrenia in economists because they combine elements of free trade, tradition- ally the *beau ideal* of most economists, and discriminating tariffs, an equally long-lived *bête noire*.

Free traders have always wished to see equal treatment of all im- ports. This is enshrined in GATT, see p. 3 above. Indeed, so strongly do some free traders feel about this point that the free trade Liberals resigned over this issue from national government in September 1932, after having accepted a general tariff in January. Yet the effect of the UK joining the EEC has been to violate this ideal. To illustrate this point, the UK car market after entry to the EEC will be considered. German cars were then allowed tariff-free entry to the UK and allowed to compete on absolutely equal terms with British cars. In other words, there had been a move towards free trade. On the other hand, until 1973 the same tariff was paid on both German and Japanese cars and in all respects they were treated alike. After entry to the EEC, Japanese cars paid a (common external) tariff of 10 per cent whereas German cars entered duty free. Hence, Japanese imports were being discrimin- ated against, compared with German ones. This is as clear a violation of free trade principles as the free competition of German and British cars is a realisation of them. So what should be the attitude of the free trader, as virtually all economists were in, say, the 1950s?

Economists have tried to answer the question by dividing the effects of a customs union into good and bad with an almost Manichaean zeal. The first to do this was Viner (1950). He did this by inventing the concepts of *trade diversion* and *trade creation*, to capture the bad and good aspects of the effect of a customs union. Viner was only interested in the impact of a customs union on the location of production, so his analysis was based on three simplifying assumptions which will be relaxed in turn in the following three sections:

1. Fixed proportions in consumption, i.e. a fixed ratio of consumption of each good to all others. This means that in partial equilibrium analysis all demand curves are perfectly inelastic.
2. Constant returns to scale.
3. All the countries forming a union are small and the resulting union is small, i.e. the terms of trade cannot be influenced by the members either prior to or after the formation of the union.

Viner's analysis incorporating these assumptions is presented in Figure 5.1. The diagram is a modification of the 'tariff triangle' introduced on p. 42 above. Prior to the union, the world price of the good is WP. A tariff T is imposed so the domestic price is (WP+T). At this price Qc is consumed. Domestic production is Qpl. Imports are Qc − Qpl, so tariff revenue is (A+B).

A customs union is then formed with another country (or countries) which can produce the good at a price PP, higher than the world price but lower than the world price plus the new common tariff (CT). (For simplicity it is assumed that the new tariff is T, otherwise a new line WP+CT can be added to Figure 5.1.) If the partner's price (PP) were to exceed WP+CT or were equal to WP, the discrimination would have no effect so the case illustrated is the only interesting one. To take a plausible example, if a German portable colour television were £105 (excluding retailer's profit and tax) and a Japanese one £100, and the tariff were 10 per cent, the illustrated case would arise. Without the discrimination, imports would be from Japan; with it, from Germany.

After the union, consumption is still Qc but domestic output falls to Qp2 and imports are now Qc−Qp2 but all come from the partner instead of the rest of the world. The effects of the change, by the usual method of analysis, are:

Figure 5.1: Viner's Analysis

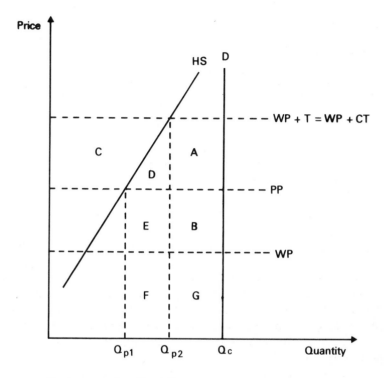

Trade created $= Q_{p2} - Q_{p1}$
Trade diverted $= Q_c - Q_{p2}$

1. the government loses the tariff revenue (A+B);
2. the producers lose profits of (C), their revenue falls by (C+D+E+F), their costs by (D+E+F);
3. consumers gain (A+D+C).

The social gain is therefore (D - B).

Viner then introduced his concepts of trade creation and diversion. He argued that trade of $Q_{p2} - Q_{p1}$ had been *created*; imports had replaced higher-cost domestic production. $Q_c - Q_{p1}$, on the other hand, represented the quantity of imports for which demand had been *diverted* from a low-cost to a higher-cost producer. The gross gain D was the gain from trade creation, the gross loss B was similarly attributable to trade diversion. These welfare effects represent the differences in the costs of production so long as WP and PP are marginal (or average) costs. (Qp1-Qp2) costs the partner (E+F) to produce compared to (D+E+F) for domestic producers, hence D is the gain from trade creation. Similarly B represents the difference between the partner's cost of producing Qc - Qp1 (B+G) and the world cost of production (G). If PP and WP are marginal costs curves (or, as for a horizontal marginal cost curve, MC= AC, average cost curves), B and D represent losses to the world. If they are not, merely to the society which joined the union; in this case more information is needed to calculate the effects on the partner country and the rest of the world.

5.3 Consumption Effects

The first of Viner's three assumptions to be relaxed was (a), the fixed proportions in consumption assumption. This was originally relaxed by Gehrels (1956) who argued that the consequent consumption effect was bound to be positive. Gehrels used a general equilibrium framework to produce this result but it is more easily studied in a partial equilibrium framework, Figure 5.2. This is just the Vinerian diagram except that the demand curve is no longer vertical. Now demand rises from Qc1 to Qc2. In consequence there is a further increase, H, in consumers' surplus; this 'consumption effect' is a further benefit of the union.

Lipsey, however (1957)(a)(b), 1960, 1970), showed that this consumption effect could go either way. Moreover, in some cases a consumption effect might produce welfare benefits in the absence of Vinerian trade creation – trade diversion need not be all bad! Lipsey's general equilibrium argument is somewhat complex, but the basic notion, that the substitution of French wine for New Zealand lamb can have a good or a bad effect on the consumer's welfare, is intuitively appealing. The reason why the consumption effect can be negative does, in fact, depend upon what is happening to the quantities of other goods consumed (and the consequent change in consumer's surpluses).

Lipsey analysis is best seen in the proof of the apparent paradox that a trade diverting customs union can be beneficial: to quote Lipsey (1957b, p. 63, in Robson (1972)):

Country A might gain by entering a customs union whose sole production effect was to divert her import trade from lower to higher

Figure 5.2: Consumption Effects

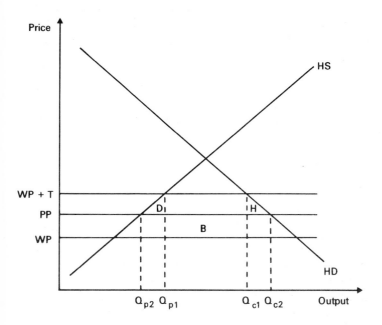

cost sources of supply.

The above conclusion may not have an immediate common sense appeal. Yet the explanation is easily seen with the help of a diagram.

The key feature of this diagram is shown in Figure 5.3. This uses a consumption possibility frontier between home produced goods and the imported good. Originally, this consumption possibility frontier is AB. Because of the tariff, consumers were not at their optimum (D); instead they are forced to the sub-optimum point 1 — see p. 34 above. The customs union changes the consumption possibility frontier to AC, reflecting the higher cost of imports, but consumers are no longer constrained to a sub-optimum, instead 2 is attainable. As drawn, 2 is clearly preferable to 1 — being on a higher indifference curve. If, however, the original consumption point had been 3, the consumers would be worse off, even though the consumption of the imported good has risen (from Q_3 to Q_2), so 'H' on Figure 5.2 exists, but it has been outweighed by the loss of surplus on the reduced consumption of other goods.

Figure 5.3: Lipsey's Analysis

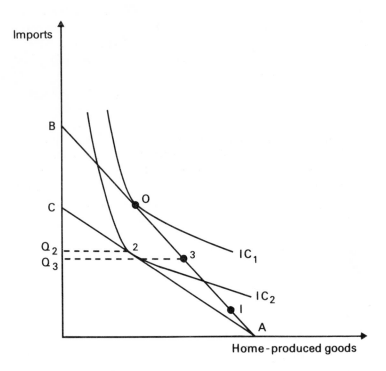

5.4 Increasing Returns to Scale and X-efficiency

That there were substantial gains from the economies of scale produced by a customs union was frequently used as an argument for British membership of the EEC prior to 1973. It was frequently linked with arguments about X-efficiency; the proposition being that the UK economy needed a good shake-up to reduce 'X-inefficiency'; the 'cold shower' or 'cold douche' argument of Harold Macmillan. Krauss (1972) cynically, but fairly, views these arguments as economic rationalisations for politically motivated decisions (p. 420) and points out the polemical value of an argument which

has become very popular both because of the large numbers it produces and because its nebulous and long-run character makes it particularly difficult to refute. (p. 432)

Krauss also points out that the evidence cited rested upon 'no theoretical rationale' in the one case and upon the weird assumption that the supply curve is the *average* cost curve, instead of the orthodox *marginal* cost curve, in the other. This preamble is necessary to explain why so much attention has been paid to what might otherwise seem to be trivial and rather pointless fields of research.

The basic proposition of the 'economies of scale' advocates that it may be better to concentrate production in an inefficient area than to produce partly in a high-cost and partly in a low-cost area (Melvin, 1969; Bhagwati, 1971). Otherwise, the economies of scale would be achieved in any case, so it is only in these circumstances that economies of scale provide an argument for a customs union.

Given that the partner country will produce a given quantity of the good anyway, it may be cheaper to produce it all there, even though at all levels of production the partner is less efficient than an alternative

Figure 5.4: Increasing Returns

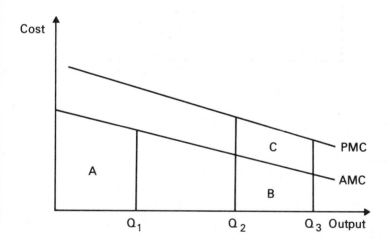

producer. Figure 5.4 reproduces this case. Partner's marginal cost curve PMC is at all levels higher than the alternative producer's (AMC). Partner will produce Q2 whatever else happens. The country joining the union wishes to import Q1. Is it better to import it from the alternative (or produce it oneself if the domestic production is the alternative) with a resource cost of A or to import it from the partner? The cost of production in the partner country is (B+C), where Q3 – Q2 = Q1. (B+C) is less than A so it is desirable to produce in a high-cost area. To use Williamson's terminology, there is a 'cost reduction' effect from concentration of production which may outweigh the 'trade suppression' effect of switching production from a low- to a high-cost area.

5.5 The Terms of Trade

Viner assumed for simplicity that both the customs union as a whole and all its members individually were small, i.e. they were unable to influence world prices. This assumption was relaxed by Viner himself later in his pioneer study (1950) and he has been followed by a host of others (see Krauss (1972)). The EEC has without doubt had a large effect on the world price of many goods, especially agricultural ones. For example, part of the CAP, see p. 68 below, has involved increased production of (beet) sugar. This, and other import restrictions, has greatly reduced world sugar prices. In consequence, the remaining imports of sugar by the EEC are much cheaper. Such effects are potentially very large, although as with all protective policies which aim to improve the terms of trade, the gains are often not realised. The beneficiaries of protection usually seek, successfully, to restrict the inflow of imports below the level which could maximise the terms of trade 'welfare' gains for their country as a whole. In fact, *pace* Pearce (1970), tariffs are rarely designed to redistribute income internationally but rather within a country. Terms of trade effects are usually a byproduct of tariffs. In any case the analysis of them is straightforward; there is no difference between the analytical tools used in the customs union case and those used in Chapters 3 and 4 above.

The problem which does arise is in deciding whether the effects are in some sense desirable. This quickly enmeshes the analyst in that notorious quagmire of compensation tests and other problems of paretian welfare economics. The concepts of welfare economics can be used in the context of the EEC, see for example Gowland in Dosser, Gowland and Hartley (1982). Nevertheless, it is probably wiser 'merely' to compute the effects of the EEC sugar policy on French farmers, UK consumers, British refiners and Australian and Jamaican producers, not to mention scores of other groups. To try to weigh these gains and losses to arrive at an overall welfare analysis is futile. Of course most people, including economists, would come to a conclusion (probably hostile to the CAP) on the basis of their value judgements but it is merely specious scientism to try to present this conclusion as a piece of economic analysis.

5.6 Some Conclusions

The orthodox theory of customs unions has been subject to a number of savage criticisms. However, none of them destroy the validity of the theory but merely stress that care must be taken in using the theory and in specifying the purposes for which it is to be used. The orthodox theory remains a useful tool; perhaps more useful than the 'new theory' discussed in 5.7 below.

The first criticism is that too much attention has been paid to the question whether 'trade diversion' could ever be a good thing. This debate often becomes a question of semantics, especially as outside the original Viner model it is often not clear to which category some changes should be assigned. However, the fact that many of the arguments have been produced within this framework does not mean that they are not useful in their own right, for example as presented above or by Krauss (1972).

The next criticism is that the 'general theory of the second best' renders any search for general conclusions vain. This nihilistic view is well founded as far as it goes. Much customs union theory is essentially piecemeal welfare economics of the sort that Lipsey and Lancaster (1956) sought to attack. It is consequently subject to the problem that an apparent welfare gain may not be a real one. (Similarly if there are 327 conditions for a welfare optimum, the achievement of 323 may not be an improvement on 322 or even none.) The indictment, however, implicitly assumes that the objective of the literature was, or should have been, to provide general conclusions about customs unions. Instead, as Lipsey made clear, and after all he was the co-discoverer of the second best, the literature was an attempt to find concepts useful in analysing what is probably the classic 'second-best' problem (1957b, p. 63 in Robson (1972)). Moreover, the literature has provided a framework for empirical analysis (see for example Krauss's survey).

The third proposition has been that the macroeconomic effects of customs unions are much more important than the resource allocation (microeconomic) effects discussed above. To take the simplest example, the increased imports whose welfare effects were applauded above may cause a balance of payments deficit which has to be cured at a much greater cost than the benefits of higher imports. This is again valid but could be applied to all microeconomic analysis. (Similarly, why bother with examining the cost effectiveness of any government expenditure? Just consider its effect on inflation and unemployment.) It is necessary to analyse the macroeconomic effects of a customs union as Godley *et al.* (1980, 1981) and El-Agraa and Jones (1981) have done. This analysis is fairly straightforward. However, the problem of deciding what would have happened otherwise is virtually insurmountable. If it is accepted that the British balance of payments would have been stronger in 1976 if the UK were not a member of the EEC, how, if at all, would Mr Healey have changed his view on the need for public expenditure cuts?

The final criticism is that customs unions, especially the EEC, have been created for political not economic reasons. This is incontravertible. Cooper and Massell have argued that there could never be an economic case for any customs union. As this is closely linked to their 'new theory' of customs unions, this view is discussed below. However, even if it were valid, it does not demonstrate the futility of orthodox theory. If a politically motivated act has economic consequences, it is necessary to examine them. This, at a minimum, will make it possible to calculate the economic cost of the policy. This may be the end of the analysis, or one may seek to try to calculate the political benefit and compare the two. To reduce the argument to a specific example, one should seek to calculate the economic consequences of membership of the EEC for the UK, even if they are adverse, and even if it were the case that no adverse economic costs would lead the UK to leave the Common Market. Even if this decision were correct, the calculation would be nevertheless important.

Hence, while all the criticisms of the orthodox theory are right in that they raise points of importance, they are wrong in that the orthodox theory is both valid and useful.

5.7 The New Theory of Customs Unions

Cooper and Massell (1965a, 1965b) sought to produce a new theory of customs unions for two reasons. One was the perceived defects of the orthodox theory (see 5.6 above) and the need to bring a political dimension into the analysis. The other was a belief that the orthodox theory was too much centred on the EEC, whereas, it then seemed, a large number of customs unions and/or free trade areas would develop in the Third World, e.g. LAFTA (Latin American Free Trade Area) and the East African Union mentioned above. With the exception of a small grouping of the statelets of Central America, none of these unions has proved successful or long-lasting; all are either defunct or moribund. However, the new theory reveals as much about the failure of these schemes as it does about their foundation.

Cooper and Massell argued that there could never be a purely economic case for a customs union. They showed that all of the benefits of a union could be achieved by a unilateral non-discriminatory tariff reduction. They then divided the effect of a union into the tariff reduction effect and a 'pure trade diversion' effect. This had achieved Viner's goal of dividing the effects of a customs union into a free trade and a protective effect (see the discussion in Krauss (1972), p. 417). However, the analysis did not show, as Cooper and Massell implied, that economic goals were not the objective, or a justification for, a customs union. It did show that a customs union could not be a first-best policy but it could still be a second-best policy. To take a specific example, in the France of the 1950s, no unilateral tariff cut was possible because no government that proposed it would have survived for more than a few days. Membership of the EEC was a feasible policy option, however. Hence a comparison of these two policies does not show that there was no economic case for French membership of the EEC. It could have been the best *possible* economic policy. Moreover, other gains as part of the EEC bargain could have outweighed the cost of 'pure trade diversion' (given the benefits to French farmers at the expense of German and Italian consumers, they probably did).

The constructive part of Cooper and Massell's analysis, the new theory itself, offers insights into Third World unions however. The key proposition is that 'two can do what one cannot', the objective being industrialisation. The underlying presumption is that Third World countries seek industrialisation as the goal of their development policy to avoid dependence on the West. However, economic independence is too expensive for any one country to achieve but a neighbouring group of countries could achieve independence. It might be that, of a group of five, A produces chemicals for all five; B steel; C cars (using B's steel) and so on. This desire for independence as a group undoubtedly inspired the abortive customs union. Equally, however, most Third World countries would rather be dependent on a far distant West, or East, than a neighbour. In the mid-1960s Kenya preferred links with the USA and the UK to ties with Tanzania and Tanzania preferred ties with China to a close relationship with Kenya. Similar examples abound. Hence it is not surprising that few such unions were long-lasting.

5.8 The Common Agricultural Policy

The EEC's common agricultural policy, CAP, is both the major achievement of the Common Maket and in most eyes its greatest shame. The CAP dominates the EEC's budget, being responsible for over 70 per cent of EEC spending, and in no other sphere of activity has the goal of a common policy achieved by common means been so successful. On the other hand, the CAP is certainly economically inefficient, arch-protectionist and does much both to impoverish the Third World and to embitter relationships between the EEC and the USA; not the best of achievements to be credited to the European ideal. The origins of the CAP are complex and go back to Pflimmin's green plan of 1949. Its most important features are a combination of high protection, usually in the form of quotas, and a guaranteed price for domestic producers; there are in fact 31 different variants of the CAP for different categories of product. An unfortunate side effect of this policy has been the reduction in efforts to modernise agriculture by most of the members – see Williams (1971) for a discussion of the changed attitude of the French government to milk producers in 1959-62, pp. 111-13. However, economic analysis of the CAP has to assume that the structure of the industry would be the same with and without the CAP.

Analysis of the CAP by Marshallian welfare area analysis is relatively straightforward and can best be illustrated by dividing the problem into two, *viz*. the effect of the quotas on the UK and the effect of the guaranteed price on the EEC as a whole. The results are presented here for a composite good, i.e. food, for which empirical data and results are taken from a variety of sources, mainly Godley (1980, 1981) and the EEC publications cited in Dosser, Gowland and Hartley (1982), Chapter 9. In the case of the UK a three-way comparison is appropriate (Figure 5.5) to compare the CAP with both free trade and with the pre-1971 'deficiency payments' system (between 1971 and 1973 an interim scheme was in force in preparation for UK entry into the EEC). The pre-1971 system was a subsidy whereby farmers were paid a guaranteed price less the average price received by all farmers (so as to maintain incentives). Thus, three prices are relevant: the world price, the UK guaranteed price, about 25 per cent higher than the world price, and the CAP price, about 90 per cent higher than the world price. A com-

Figure 5.5: CAP: Impact on the UK

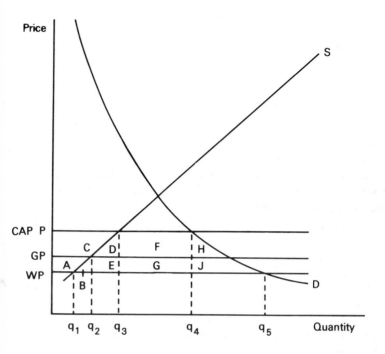

parison of free trade and the UK system is simple as domestic consumption is q_5 in both cases but domestic output rises from q_1 to q_2. Farmers gain A (revenue rises by A + B + K, but costs rise by K). The government pays out (A + B) as a subsidy to the farmers; (A + B) was in practice variable but averaged about £300 million in the late 1960s. Hence the consequences of the UK system were to impose a social cost of 'B' (the production effect); to benefit farmers at the expense of taxpayers and to reduce imports by ($q_2 - q_1$). The effect of the CAP was to raise price to CAP P so domestic consumption fell to q_4 and domestic output rose to q_3. There is no tariff revenue as the protection is by quota so the only relevant effects are on producers and consumers. Compared to either free trade or the old UK system, consumers lose (A + B + C + D + E + F + G + H + J), about £3000 million in 1980. Producers gain C compared to the UK system (£1000 million) and (A + C) compared to free trade. The government gains under the CAP (compared to the subsidy system) by not having to pay out the subsidy, i.e. (A + B). Adding all the relevant areas up, the social cost of the CAP is (D + E + F

+ G + H + J) compared to the pre-1971 system. This area was equivalent to about £1500 million in 1980. The cost of the CAP is even higher in comparison to free trade, by 'B'.

Figure 5.6: CAP: EEC as a Whole

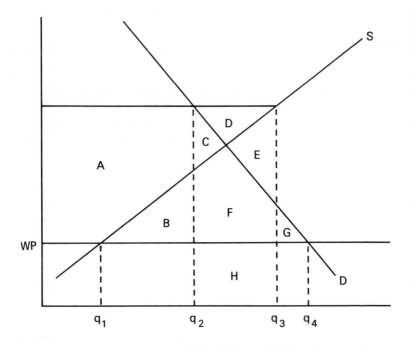

However, the total cost of the CAP is still higher because the payment to the EEC to finance the guaranteed price system has to be added. This is about £1000 million, so the total cost to the UK of the CAP is about £2500 million, about half of which is paid in foreign exchange. The derivation of this payment is shown in Figure 5.6, the food market for the EEC as a whole. D is the demand curve by EEC citizens for food, less the quota permitted by the CAP (if any). A further consequence of the CAP is that consumers pay more for this but this effect is not illustrated. The rest of the analysis is standard, except that output at the CAP price exceeds EEC demand. The EEC is committed to purchasing this excess supply at the price CAP P. EEC demand is q_2 compared to q_4 under free trade so consumers lose (A + B + C + F + G). Farmers sell q_2 to consumers but their remaining output (q_3 - q_2) is bought by the EEC, through the appropriate agency.

Farmers, therefore, gain $(A + C + D)$. The EEC has purchased $(q_3 - q_2)$ of food for which it has paid $(C + D + E + F + H)$. It has to store it — the famous butter mountain, wine lake, etc. It may dispose of it in various ways. The most commonly used has been to sell the surplus at less than WP to the USSR but the range of methods of disposal is truly ingenious. The simplest method for analytical purposes is to assume that it is sold at the world price — the best from the CAP point of view and in some metaphysical sense its value. In this case the loss to EEC governments would be $(C + D + E + F)$, of which the UK share is the £1000 million referred to above. The total welfare cost of the CAP is $(B + C + E + G + 2F)$; the double appearance of F is anomalous but reflects the double cost involved in buying from a higher-cost producer and then being prevented from consuming the good.

The CAP is a rather mundane topic upon which to conclude analysis of customs unions. In fact, it is appropriate in that the message of the theory of customs unions is that there are no general rules, that all results have to be painstakingly derived. This complements the history of the EEC which reveals that hard bargaining by nation states with (enlightened) self-interest is not the destruction of the European ideal but the only means by which the ideal can be salvaged — if indeed it can be.

6 THE TRADITIONAL BALANCE OF PAYMENTS THEORY

6.1 Balance of Payments Theory: An Introduction

In the next three chapters various alternative methods of analysing the balance of payments are presented. The different theories seek to explain different aspects of the balance of payments, so they are to a considerable extent complementary rather than competitive. The elasticities, or traditional, approach seeks to explain the balance of trade; the Keynesian theories (Chapter 6) the current balance; the monetary theory (Chapter 7) the overall balance (the meaning of the balance of payments and of these concepts is explained in sections 6.2 and 6.3). The theories are complementary in another sense. The traditional theory is a microeconomic theory of adjustment in the goods market; the Keynesian theory a macroeconoimic theory in the goods market and the monetary theory a theory of disequilibrium in the money market. Balance of payments analysis needs to comprise all these elements but it is often more convenient to have three separate tools of analysis rather than a general model incorporating all three. Of course, 'after we have reached a provisional conclusion by isolating the complicating factors one by one we then have to go back on ourselves and allow, as well as we can, for the probable interaction of the factors among themselves. This is the nature of economic thinking.' As this comment of Keynes, which was endorsed by Friedman, suggests, this is the standard approach in economic analysis to a potentially complex problem (Keynes (1936), p. 297, cited by Friedman in Gordon (1974), p. 150).

6.2: Some Concepts

The balance of payments is strictly an accounting term used to describe a record of all of the transactions between one country and the rest of the world. As in all accounting records, transactions are recorded in two ways so that (unless mistakes are made) the total calculated from each method must be the same, i.e. the account must balance. Alternatively, the total derived by one method can be subtracted from that derived by the other. The result of this subtraction must be zero. As a consequence of such accounting conventions, *any* balance of payments must balance. A balance of payments problem is, accordingly, a problem about *how* the balance of payments balances. In principle a balance of payments could be constructed for an individual, a company or an area just as easily as for a country. It is a crucial feature of any balance of payments that it is a record of cash inflows and outflows. Companies frequently produce such statements which are a key tool of modern management. Instead of being called a balance of payments they are called either a cash flow account or a sources and uses of funds statement.

To illustrate the nature of a balance of payments, Table 6.1 shows the sources and uses of funds of an imaginary student. Version A simply lists his sources of funds and how he has used them. However, we might decide to group transactions which seem similar. Thus his sources of funds might be grouped into income and borrowing; his expenditure into that which involves the acquisition of an asset and the rest, i.e. current expenditure. One can also regard the use of funds as a negative source and so arrive at version B. This grouping is arbitrary. For example, one might have classed the purchase of books as a purchase of assets, with the car, rather than current expenditure with the alcohol, rent, etc. The choice of headings is also arbitrary, for example one might alternatively have divided sources into public sector, family and corporate sector. This arbitrariness is common to all balance of payments accounts.

One might then group some sources and some uses of funds having something in common. For example, the borrowing and car purchase might be regarded as having something in common with each other, as both are capital transactions while income and the current expenditure can be grouped as current transactions. This grouping is again arbitrary or rather should be a consequence of the purpose for which the account is to be used. No grouping is 'right' or 'wrong'. It is merely more or less useful. The balance of payments statistics used in the UK reflect the CSO's views of what is the most useful method of presentation; this view has changed several times in the last 30 years.

The final presentation has two features of considerable importance.

1. Whilst the total of the account must be zero, it is possible, indeed likely, that each section will show either a net contribution to the student's funds or a net drain on them. These are called either surpluses or deficits respectively.

Hence the student has a current transactions balance of payments

Table 6.1: A Student's Balance of Payments

A	Sources of funds			Uses of funds	
S1	Grant	£1500	U1	Rent	£1000
S2	Income from		U2	Food	£ 990
	vacation jobs	£1000	U3	Books	£ 10
S3	Borrowing	£1000	U4	Alcohol	£ 500
	from bank		U5	Other recurrent	£1000
S4	Borrowing	£ 500		expenditure	
	from parents		U6	Purchase of car	£1000
		£4000			£4000
B			Net source (use −)		
B1	Income		£2500 (i.e. S1 + S2)		
B2	Borrowing		£1500 (i.e. S3 + S4)		
B3	Current expenditure		− £3000 (i.e. U1 + U2 + U3 + U4 + U5)		
B4	Purchase of asset (car)		− £1000 (i.e. U6)		
			000		
C	Current transactions (B1 + B3)		− £ 500		
	Capital transactions (B2 + B4)		+ £ 500		
			000		

deficit of £500, because his current expenditure exceeds his income.

2. Any balance of payments deficit means that some category of transaction has made a net contribution to the individual's funds. *An increase in one's holdings of assets is a balance of payments deficit* because it involves the use of funds. Borrowing is a surplus because it entails the acquisition of funds.

Both features are true of all balance of payments accounts. They must *balance* in the sense that the final total must be zero. However, they can be divided into components, such as current and capital, which must sum to zero. These are almost certain to show either a surplus or a deficit. These surpluses or deficits may be viewed as policy problems. In practice, current transactions deficits are often so regarded. Indeed in the UK from 1945 to 1972 they were viewed as the major problem of economic policy. Nevertheless, it is worth stressing that it is only components of the balance of payments which can show deficits or surpluses; the overall account must balance. Thus a balance of payments problem is really a problem of the composition of the balance of payments.

6.3 The UK Balance of Payments

Exports and imports are the two best-known transactions with the overseas sector and comprise those sales to foreign residents (exports) and purchases from them (imports), which are included in the national income accounts. However, the usual method of presenting the UK balance of payments both subdivides these categories and includes several others.

The UK balance of payments is divided in two main sections: the current account, which showed a surplus of £3206 million in 1980, and the capital account which showed a deficit of £2790 million (an item grouping errors and omissions, called the balancing item, ensures that the account balanced). The current account in turn is subdivided into:

Table 6.2: The UK Current Account, 1980

Visible trade			
		(£m)	
Exports		47,389	
Imports		− 46,211	
Visible balance		+ 1,178	
Services			
	Credit	Debit	Balance
General government	397	−1,188	−791
Sea transport	3,816	−3,681	+135
Travel	2,965	−2,757	+208
Finance	n/a	n/a	+1,595
Other	4,826	2,180	+646
	15,809	11,621	+3,285
Interest, Profit and Dividends			
	Receipts	Payments	Balance
General government	943	1,598	+655
Private sector (including public corporations)	7,261	6,644	−617
Transfers			
General government	958	2,790	−1,832
Private	793	1,083	−290
Invisible: Consolidated			
Credits		25,764	
Debits		23,736	
Invisible balance		+2,028	
Current Balance		+3,206	

6.3.1 Visible Trade

This item represents trade in goods, of which £47,389 million were exported and £46,211 million imported in 1980. This was only the eighth year since the end of the Napoleonic wars when exports of goods exceeded imports, although similar surpluses were earned in 1981 and 1982 for which complete figures are not available.

6.3.2 Invisible Trade

'Invisibles' comprise three items; trade in services, interest profit and dividends and transfers.

6.3.3 Services

Of these travel is the best known and shipping and finance are the largest. A Briton taking a holiday abroad is importing in just the same way as if he/she purchases foreign goods and consumes them in the UK. A British insurance company selling a policy to an American is exporting in just the same way as a seller of aircraft. Altogether in 1980 services showed a surplus of £3285 million, most of it earned by the City.

6.3.4 Interest, Profit and Dividends

This item, which showed a small deficit in 1980, reflects income received from foreign loans and investments and income paid to foreign investors in the UK, whether holders of UK securities or real assets (such as Ford). Normally the private sector earns a large surplus but the public sector makes large payments, so the net figure is small.

6.3.5 Transfers

This item includes all those current transactions which are, in effect, gifts, since the person paying the money receives nothing in exchange (at least directly). This item showed a deficit of £2122 million in 1980. Part of this represented private transfers − gifts to relatives abroad, charitable donations and so on. However, the bulk represented government transfers of which contributions to the EEC were the largest, over £1500 million, net of refunds.

The capital account includes real investment, or *direct* investment, in land, factories, etc. and *portfolio* investment in securities, shares, bonds, etc. Most of this investment is long term but there are also very large quantities of short-term capital transactions. Some, both official and private, are loans designed to finance the purchase of current goods and services, but large quantities of short-term deposits are made both in and by the UK only in response to the attractiveness of the deposit. This means that there are often very large movements of capital when interest rates change or when there are fears that a currency's value will fall (see p. 133 below). The capital account also includes official financing transactions such as changes in the reserves. The government holds a large stock of foreign currency which is used for various purposes, such as to influence the exchange rate (see p. 160 below). This stock is called the reserves and an addition to it — a purchase of foreign currency by the government — is a deficit, because it represents a use of funds. The official transactions are usually presented as the item needed to meet the 'balance for official settlement' or 'total currency flow'.

The current account, plus all capital transactions other than the official financing ones, is often called the *overall* balance. If the short-term capital investments described above are excluded, it is called the basic *balance*. Of course items in different sections of the balance of payments may be related. If an aeroplane is purchased from an American firm it will usually arrange a subsidised loan as part of the deal. The aircraft would appear in the current account, the loan in the capital account.

6.4 The Elasticities Model

The traditional approach to the analysis of the balance of payments is embodied in the elasticities model. This model seeks to explain the balance of trade, i.e. exports and imports, by a microeconomic approach which focuses on the choice between domestic and foreign goods. The quantity of UK imports is determined by UK residents choosing to buy foreign, rather than British, goods and services and exports by foreign residents making the opposite choice. As in all elementary (partial analytic) microeconomies, it is assumed that price is the main determinant of this choice. Thus the relative price of British and foreign goods and services will determine the quantities of each purchased; of course, this is only true when a number of other factors are held constant; when these are not constant, the defects of the theory discussed in section 6.5 arise.

Hence the theory is based on the premise that exports and imports are determined by relative prices. The relative price of British and, say, American goods is determined both by their absolute prices and by the exchange rate. To take a specific example: a china beaker costs £1 in York. Its American equivalent costs $3 in New York. The relative price of the two depends on the exchange rate. If the rate were $1.50 = £1, the American beaker would cost £2 and be more expensive. Hence, Americans would import beakers from York. On the other hand, if the exchange rate were $3, then both would cost £1 and no trade would take place. If the rate were any higher, it would pay Britons to import beakers from New York, for example if the rate were $6 the sterling price of the American beaker would be 50p. Thus the elasticities model argues that the quantity of exports and imports will depend upon domestic prices, foreign prices and the exchange rate.

Before continuing with the theory, it is worth noting that there are two alternative links between these three besides the elasticities model. One is the *purchasing power parity* theory. This argues that it is the exchange rate which adjusts, so that prices will be the same in both countries. Hence, in my example, the exchange rate will be $3 so that the £1 and the $3 it buys will both purchase the same quantity of goods, for example one beaker. A second, more modern argument is that the world price and the exchange rate determine domestic prices. In the above example, if the exchange rate were $2, then the sterling price of an American beaker would be $1.50. In this case, no UK producer has any reason to sell at any price less than £1.50, nor can he sell at any price above £1.50, so his price will be £1.50. This is an extension of the 'small country' assumption used, for example, in the tariff analysis above.

Relative prices can change either as a result of a change in the exchange rate or of a change in absolute prices, both domestic and foreign. These are often combined into an index of competitiveness. UK competitiveness will improve, in practice, if UK prices rise by less than foreign ones or if the exchange rate falls. When the exchange rate changes so that the pound buys less dollars this is called a depreciation. In some circumstances this change can be brought about by official action and is called devaluation (see p. 41 below). According to the theory, an improvement in competitiveness must lead to a rise in the *volume* of exports or a fall in the *volume* of imports (or both), i.e. demand curves slope downwards. However, one is interested in the *value* of exports, as well as the *volume*. For example, if five beakers were sold at 50p each instead of three at £1 each, then one would probably think that this was a *fall* in exports from £3 to £2.50, i.e. in value, not a rise from three to five beakers, i.e. in volume. To calculate the change in value, one needs to know the price elasticities of exports and imports; hence the name of the theory. Export revenue will rise (in pounds) if the elasticity exceeds unity, and so on as in elementary price theory.

The essence of the theory is embodied in the famous Marshall-Lerner condition:

> an improvement in competitiveness will improve the balance of payments if and only if the sum of the price elasticities of demand for imports by residents and of exports by non-residents exceeds unity (ignoring the negative signs of the elasticities).

Improvement in the balance of payments is taken to mean a smaller (current account) deficit or a larger surplus. Usually an improvement in competitiveness is achieved by a variation in the exchange rate so the condition is often stated using depreciation or devaluation instead of change in competitiveness. The crucial feature of the condition is that it is the *sum* of the elasticities which must exceed one, not each elasticity separately. Hence it is possible for both exports and imports to be price inelastic but for the condition to be satisfied, e.g. if both elasticities are equal to (–) 0.7.

It is necessary to explain in some detail why this is so. The simplest way to do this emphasises that the balance of payments can be measured in either foreign currency or domestic currency, hereafter dollars and pounds. An improvement in UK competitiveness, in this case a depreciation of sterling, will mean that the dollar price of exports falls and the sterling price of imports rises, whereas the sterling price of exports is unchanged and so is the foreign currency price of imports. This is because the change in the exchange rate has not affected the price measured in the relevant domestic currency but it has affected the price in the other currency.

If the balance of payments is measured in *sterling*, the following is true. The sterling price of exports is unchanged (even though foreigners pay less in their own currency) so the value of exports cannot fall; in fact it is almost certain to rise as volume will rise unless the elasticity is equal to zero. This assumption, however, will be made. If the export elasticity is zero, the value of exports will be unchanged. In this case, the change in the value of imports will determine what happens to the balance of payments. As the sterling price of imports has risen, the sterling value of imports will fall so long as their elasticity of demand exceeds one. In other words, *a depreciation*, or rather improvement in competitiveness, *will lead to an improvement in the balance of payments so long as the import elasticity exceeds one, even if the export elasticity is zero*.

If the balance of payments is measured in foreign currency, the converse argument is true. The price of imports in dollars is unchanged so their value cannot rise. (In fact, as the sterling price is higher, it is almost certain to fall.) If the import elasticity is zero, the value will be unchanged. In this case, the effect of the depreciation on the balance of payments will depend upon the effect of the lower foreign currency price of exports. It is obvious that there will be an increase in the value of exports so long as the export elasticity exceeds unity. Thus, *even if the import elasticity is zero, a depreciation will improve the balance of payments if and only if the export elasticity is greater than one.*

It is necessary to make a drastic simplifying assumption to derive the Marshall-Lerner condition from the two italicised propositions above. This is that the balance of payments is initially in balance. In this case an improvement in the balance of payments in either sterling or dollars implies an improvement in the other. Therefore, *either* an export *or* an import elasticity greater than unity is a sufficient condition for a depreciation to improve the balance of payments, even if the other is equal to zero. Moreover, if the balance of payments is in balance, i.e. exports are equal to imports, then an import elasticity of (-) ½ will have exactly the same impact on the balance of payments as an export elasticity of (-) ½ (as the one will reduce imports by as much as the other will increase exports). Hence if both elasticities are equal to (-) ½, the effect will be the same as if either is equal to one and the other to zero. The same is true of any other pair of elasticities which add up to one. Hence, so long as the sum of elasticities exceeds unity, then an improvement in competitiveness will improve the balance of payments, i.e. the Marshall-Lerner condition. However, to show this a number of simplifying assumptions have been explicitly and implicitly made. The deficiencies and limitations of Marshall-Lerner are considered in the next section and all stem from these. However, the basic theory is simple: *relative prices (competitiveness) determines the balance of payments, with an improvement in competitiveness leading to an improvement in the balance of payments so long as the Marshall-Lerner condition is satisfied.*

6.5 The Deficiencies of the Marshall-Lerner Condition

6.5.1 Balanced Payments Assumption

The first of the limitations of the Marshall-Lerner condition stems from the assumption that the (current account of the) balance of payments is in balance initially. Otherwise the condition is neither sufficient nor necessary for an improvement in competitiveness. This seems a very restrictive assumption as the balance of payments is very rarely in balance and, almost by definition, never so when there is a balance of payments problem. However, this is less restrictive than it seems, as in this case the Marshall-Lerner condition is replaced by the alternative sufficient condition that the *weighted* sum of the elasticities should exceed one, with the weights proportional to the value of exports and imports. In effect the simple Marshall-Lerner condition is equivalent to the proposition that an unweighted, or equally weighted, sum of the elasticities should exceed unity.

A further complication arises because it is possible for a balance of payments to improve in foreign currency but not in pounds or vice versa. For example, if the original deficit were £400 million and the exchange rate $2 = £1, the deficit would be $800 million. If after a depreciation to $1 = £1 the deficit were £600 million or $600 million this could be viewed as an improvement (in dollars) or a worsening (in sterling). The minimum necessary condition is slightly different according to which currency the deficit/surplus is measured in.

Nevertheless, whilst the Marshall-Lerner condition itself is no longer appropriate, there is always an amended elasticity condition which avoids the drastic balanced payments assumption.

6.5.2 Aggregation, Practical Problems and Elasticity Pessimism

The analysis in section 6.4 implicitly assumed that there was only one good exported and imported. This is clearly absurd; the UK exports and imports several hundred thousand different goods. However, even with two goods the aggregation problem would arise; in some ways it is a variant of the index number problem.

If the UK imported two goods, one with an elasticity of (-) 0.1 and one with an elasticity of (-) 0.6, what elasticity is relevant to the Marshall-Lerner or similar formulae? Clearly one needs some weighted average of 0.1 and 0.6, but there is no correct set of weights. The relative volume, or value, of imports (or consumption?) offer some possible answers but each level of income and price offers a different answer. In theory there is no solution to the aggregation problem. In practice, national income-based data are used as if they applied to a single good.

Perhaps more seriously, the plethora of goods makes it very hard indeed to estimate elasticities at either the level of the aggregate or at that of the individual good. It is virtually impossible to calculate the correct relative price. All the usual econometric problems are present (see p. 14 above). Hence it has proved difficult to estimate whether or not the Marshall-Lerner condition and its variants is satisfied. However, the evidence suggests that 'elasticity pessimism' may well be justified, that the values may be very low indeed, or at least so close to a sum of unity that it is not clear whether or not the condition is fulfilled (see Appendix).

6.5.3 Supply Side Factors

The Marshall-Lerner condition implicitly assumes that all supply elasticities are equal to infinity or, to put it less formally, that there are no supply constraints on the volume of trade. This is a serious limitation, and so a major justification for the absorption approach in which these are central (see Chapter 7). It is very unlikely that British producers could increase their output by very much in response to an increase in foreign demand. Almost certainly, they would choose to increase price as well as, or instead of, output. In addition, there is evidence that the state of the domestic market influences behaviour in the export market. In other words, whilst Marshall-Lerner implicitly assumes a perfectly elastic supply curve which is more or less stable, in the real world the supply of UK exports is neither stable nor very elastic.

There are two approaches to this problem; one is to try to expand the condition to include supply elasticities. Unfortunately the resulting conditions are horrifically complex and no two advanced textbooks seem to agree on what the condition would be.[2] Moreover, one should accept that elasticity analysis is about demand and incorporate this into a broader analysis. So many factors are left out by Marshall-Lerner, including any other impact of changed competitiveness on the domestic economy, that this seems to be the better solution. Marshall-Lerner can never provide a complete balance of payments model, but it is still of value (see section 6.6 below).

6.5.4. Income Effects

The major factor missing in the elasticities analysis is income effects; they are implicitly assumed away (i.e. it is partial analysis). So the Marshall-Lerner condition assumes that the income elasticity of demand for *all* goods is zero. This is so implausible that it has led to the development of the alternative macroeconomic models of the balance of payments, discussed in Chapters 7 and 8. The sort of mechanism ignored by Marshall-Lerner includes such processes as:

1. a change in relative prices increase exports,
2. the increase in exports generates an increase in income;
3. the higher level of income leads to more imports.

This latter increase in imports can be such that there is no improvement in the balance of payments despite the rise in exports.

The following example, using the elementary multiplier-accelerator model of 'A' level and first-year macroeconomics courses, illustrates the potential impact of income effects. In a simple economy:

X = 100	M = 0.2Y
I = 100+0.3Y	T = 0.1Y
G = 100	S = 0.1Y (where X = exports, etc.)

As can be easily calculated, the equilibrium level of income is 3000. As imports will, therefore, be 600, there will be a balance of payments deficit of 500.

For simplicity it will be assumed that the price elasticity of demand for imports is 0, but that a 5 per cent devaluation, or other improvement in competitiveness, will lead to a 500 per cent increase in the level of exports. In other words, the Marshall-Lerner condition is satisfied many times over (the sum of elasticities is over 30). After the devaluation

X = 600 (and all the other variables as above)

The new equilibrium level of income is 8000. Imports are now 1600, so the balance of payments deficit is 1000. In other words, although the Marshall-Lerner condition is satisfied, an improvement in competitiveness has led to a doubling of the deficit.

The above example suggests that one needs to look at two distinct influences on the balance of payments:

1. the impact of a change in competitiveness on the balance of payments if income were held constant. This change (hereafter B) is given by the elasticities model: this was the increase in exports (500) in the above examples but could also include a fall in the average propensity to import.
2. the rise in imports generated by the higher level of income. The second of these is equal to the marginal propensity to import (m) multiplied by the change in income. Hence one must calculate the

change in income. This is equal to the multiplier times the increase in injections, as in any Keynesian system. This increase in injections is B (the change in the balance of payments holding income constant). This can be checked by re-examining the example above, where it can be seen that the increase in exports is the injection which raises income from 3000 to 8000. Hence, to set it out more formally, the total effect of a change in competitiveness is equal to

$$= B - B.m.k$$

where k is the multiplier (Bmk gives the generated rise in imports)

$$= B (1 - mk).$$

As B will be positive for an improvement in competitiveness so long as the modified Marshall-Lerner condition is satisfied, then additional conditions can be derived. If $mk > 1$, then the generated effect on imports outweighs the change implied by the Marshall-Lerner condition. However, so long as $mk < 1$, then an improvement in competiveness will lead to an improvement in the balance of payments. This consideration of income effects produces two conclusions; the additional condition to complement Marshall-Lerner and the idea that changes in competitiveness influence income. The latter will be considered further in the next section and in Chapter 10.

Table 6.3: Effect on Balance of Payments of Exchange Rate Changes

	Change in balance of payments	Change in exchange rate (%)
USA (1977-9)	+ $ 16 bn	– 11.3
Japan (1977-9)	– $ 9 bn	+ 15.9 [1]
Germany (1977-9)	– $ 6 bn	+ 13.3
Italy (1974-8)	+ $ 6½ bn	– 31.2
UK (1974-7)	+ $ 21½ bn	– 25.8
UK (1977-9)	– $ 5 bn	+ 9.1

Source: Allen, W.A. 'Exchange Rates and Balance of Payments Adjustment — General Principles and Some Recent Experiences', *BIS Working Paper No. 3.*

6.6 The Value of Marshall-Lerner

Opinion is divided about the relevance of Marshall-Lerner, or competitiveness, to the balance of payments. On the one hand, some economists believe that competitiveness is a major determinant of the balance of payments; for example Allen's estimates shown in Table 6.3. On the other hand, the doyen of British economics, Johnson, could write:

> It should be emphasised that the analysis of the effects of a devaluation is *completely* independent of *any* critical magnitude condition applying to the elasticities of international demand. The relevant stability condition is . . . monetary theoretic' (Johnson, in Frenkel and Johnson, p. 275)

> The familiar elasticity condition (sum-of-the-elasticities-of-demand-greater-than-unity) . . . is completely irrelevant. (*Ibid.*, p. 281)

However, it is clear, that the elasticities approach in general, and modified Marshall-Lerner in particular, can be relevant to the analysis of inflation and unemployment. The full argument is developed below, p. 138 , but both 'competitiveness' and 'exchange rate' are regarded as having their major impact, possibly their only impact, on the level of domestic income. Thus a depreciation is seen as a way of reducing unemployment and an appreciation of reducing inflation. Hence the income effect, whose size does depend in part on Marshall-Lerner analysis, is not an unwelcome by-product but the object of the policy. In November 1982, the Labour Party's Shadow Chancellor, Peter Shore, advocated a 30 per cent depreciation of sterling as a means of reducing unemployment. Similarly, exogenous changes in competitiveness have also been sought, e.g. by incomes policy, as a means to reduce unemployment. In some models, e.g. the Bank of England one (Bank (1979)), such effects are of crucial importance.

Appendix A: Price and International Competitiveness

Most presentations of international trade theory implicitly assume that price is the major influence on potential purchasers and that trade theory should therefore concentrate on showing why prices might differ between different countries, to establish the existence or optimality of trade. Similarly, balance of payments theories concentrated on the impact of price on volume. Strictly, these analyses need not imply that the price elasticities of international trade are high but most writers and students assumed they were until the 1950s when efforts to estimate them commenced. These results were alleged to show 'elasticity pessimism' in that the elasticities were smaller than anticipated — about 1.5 to 2. In the ensuing 30 years estimates of elasticities have become ever lower, so the current consensus is that elasticities are unitary or less.

There are a large number of major problems that must be surmounted before elasticities can be estimated. The first is the poor quality of the data. It is symptomatic of the poor quality of the data that measured world exports are 5 per cent less than world imports, even though one would expect the bias to be to underestimate imports since smuggled goods often appear in export statistics but never in import data, by definition. Moreover, it is very hard to calculate which price is relevant to which goods especially when aggregate data is used. Even where reliable data is available researchers have faced virtually all known econometric problems in their work. Technicalities aside, the major problem has been to isolate the effect of price changes from those of the other factors at work. Usually estimation of price elasticities has been by regression analysis using time series data.

A particular problem facing international economists has been the estimation of lagged relationships. It is usually argued that past as well as present prices should influence trade flows. This is partly because of *contractual commitments*. If someone agreed to buy x tons of coal per year from the UK for ten years in 1977, they would be influenced by 1977 prices (and their expectations) but deliveries will continue until 1987. Hence UK coal exports today would depend in part upon 1977 prices as well as today's. Another reason is *delivery lags*. There is often a substantial gap between the placing of an order and the delivery of a good. The observed flow is of deliveries but presumably the relevant price which influenced the decision was the one prevailing when the order was placed.

The techniques needed to estimate such lagged relationships are complicated, but the crucial problem is that one can estimate a short lag with a low elasticity or a higher elasticity but one which takes years to work through. Statistical methodology cannot satisfactorily determine which is right. The UK Treasury model of exports at one time had a high elasticity (of - 1.6) but a 26 quarter lag. Critics argued that this strained plausibility. In brief, empirical estimation of the effects of trade flows has been successful in showing that elasticities are not high but not successful in establishing how low.

Appendix B: Marshall-Lerner and Income Effects — a Diagrammatic Presentation

A demand curve shows the relationship between price and the desired quantity purchased. The change in total revenue in equilibrium when price changes depends upon the elasticity of the demand curve. It is, however, possible to use instead the concept of an expenditure function — i.e. price times quantity — and to show how this changes when price changes. This is shown in Figure 6.1 (a). When elasticity is greater than unity this slopes downwards and vice versa. The same can be done for the balance of payments which represents expenditure on imports net of exports. This can be negative, i.e. there can be a surplus. Hence, Figure 6.1 (b) shows the effect of changes in the relative price of imports on net expenditure on imports, i.e. on the balance of payments, when GDP is constant. So long as the (modified) Marshall-Lerner condition is satisfied, this will slope downwards from left to right — and this is the relevance of the condition.

If income were constant, a rise in the relative price of imports would improve the balance of payments, e.g. a depreciation that raised the relative price of imports from p_1 to p_2 would improve the balance of payments by AB. However, AB is an injection which necessarily increases income and so shifts the expenditure function from E_1 to E_2, as more is demanded at each level of income and price so expenditure rises. The shift may be such that the total effect on the balance of payments is negative, positive or zero. The shift is AB. MPM. multiplier (k) as on p. 82 above, so it is easy to see that there will be an improvement only if MPM.k $<$ 1. (NB when there are no income effects MPM = 0, so MPM. k equals zero.)

Notes

1. The use of the word 'traditional' is open to the question 'What tradition?', especially in view of the alternative tradition cited by Frenkel and Johnson (1976, Chapter 1). Nevertheless, the word traditional is a useful description of the mainstream textbook orthodoxy of the 1950s and 1960s.

2. The most comprehensive incorporation of supply elasticities was by Stern (1973). His formula required that

Figure 6.1: Marshall-Lerner

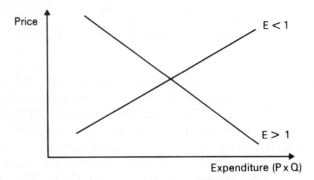

a) Expenditure functions

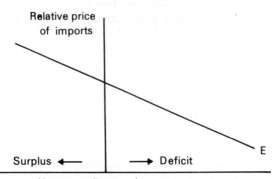

b) Marshall - Lerner satisfied

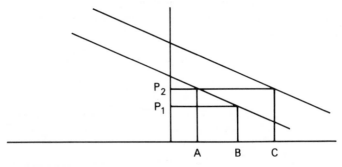

c) Income effects

$$X \; \frac{\Sigma x - 1}{1 + \dfrac{\Sigma x}{Sx}} \; + M \; \frac{\Sigma m \, (1 + \frac{1}{Sm})}{\dfrac{\Sigma m}{S\,m} + 1} \; > 0$$

for a depreciation to improve the balance of payments where X and M are the initial values of exports and imports, Sx and Sm the supply elasticities and Σx and Σm the demand elasticities of exports and imports respectively.

Table 6.4 summarises his results.

Table 6.4: Stern's Results

	Demand elasticities	Supply elasticities	Effect on: Terms of trade	Balance of trade
1	Both high and sum 1	Both high	Moderate worsening or improvement[a]	Improvement
2	Both high and sum 1	Both low	Improvement[b]	Improvement
3	Both low and sum 1	Both high	Worsening	Worsening
4	Both low and sum 1	Both low	Improvement[b]	Improvement[b]

Notes: (a) depends on whether the product of the supply elasticities is greater or less than the product of the demand elasticities; (b) if supply elasticities are sufficiently small in relation to the demand elasticities.

7 KEYNESIAN BALANCE OF PAYMENTS THEORIES

7.1 The Absorption Model

The original Keynesian balance of payments theory was the absorption model developed by Alexander, of the IMF, in the early 1950s. As in all Keynesian models, the balance of payments, on current account, is analysed as a macroeconomic phenomenon in the goods market. The (current account) balance of payments will necessarily equal the difference between aggregate domestic output and aggregate domestic expenditure (with a surplus if output is larger and vice versa). This conclusion follows from a manipulation of the basic national income identity, which is that there are three ways of measuring national income: income, output (O) and expenditure (E), of which only the latter two are relevant here.

$$O = E \qquad (7.1)$$

The expenditure is defined as the sum of consumers' expenditure (C), investment (I), government expenditure (G) and exports (X) less imports (M).

$$E = C + I + G + X - M \qquad (7.2)$$

(7.2) can be substituted into (7.1) to give

$$O = C + I + G + X - M \qquad (7.3)$$

(7.3) can be arranged as

$$X - M = O - (C + I + G) \qquad (7.4)$$

This piece of manipulation is the absorption approach. Alexander called $(C + I + G)$ absorption rather than the more usual 'total domestic expenditure'. The implication of the approach is simple. One should not seek to explain the balance of payments directly, rather one should look at the determinants of output and total domestic expenditure and the balance of payments will be automatically defined as a residual. Competitiveness, the exchange rate and any other factor will matter only in so far as it influences either TDE or output. These effects may be substantial or small but, critically, they may be apparently perverse. A devaluation will increase expenditure, and may even reduce output (or output may already be at a maximum). In this case, a devaluation would worsen the balance of payments, irrespective of the size of elasticities.

It is important to realise how neatly the absorption model complements the elasticities approach. The traditional approach ignored supply side effects (6.5.3) and income effects (6.5.4). The absorption approach looks only at these two effects. The two approaches can be combined. It is also interesting to note that two of the basic implications of this approach, but not the conclusion, are included in the most elementary textbooks. It is common to see statements like

1. deflation can improve the balance of payments.

2. devaluation can improve the balance of payments but only if it is 'made to work' by deflation. (Strictly, this assumes that output is fixed.)

However, the obvious conclusion is not drawn.

3. the balance of payments can only be improved if there is deflation. ('Recognition of this point may be regarded as the fundamental contribution of the absorption approach though none of the authors cited seems to have appreciated all its implications' (Johnson, in Frenkel and Johnson (1970), p. 59).)

These three statements, and the many qualifications to them, are all drawn from the absorption model, as will be demonstrated. (1) is very simple. Deflation lowers TDE so it will improve the balance of payments. However, it will reduce output as well, so the improvement in the balance of payments will be less than the reduction in expenditure. As the absorption approach is the open economy version of the Keynesian model, this is usually illustrated by an analysis in which output is demand-determined. In this case output is $X + (1 - m)(C + I + G)$, where m is the marginal propensity to import, i.e. output is that which is necessary to satisfy export demand plus the part of home demand not spent on imports. In this case the fall in output is $(1 - m)$ times the fall in expenditure; exports are taken to be exogenous. This fall in output is obviously less than the fall in expenditure (unless m is negative). The improvement in the balance of payments is m times (the fall in expenditure).

In effect, a reduction in (C + I + G) automatically reduces imports and so improves the balance of payments. This conclusion is perhaps obvious and the analysis simplistic, but like so many other obvious facts, it took economists to point it out! (In such models, it is necessary for m to be less than 1 otherwise the model is unstable; this is not demonstrated as the model is only illustrative and it is difficult to see how m could exceed 1, so long as other influences are properly specified.)

The next statements, (2) and (3) above, are very easy to demonstrate. *So long as output is fixed*, an improvement in the balance of payments must be accompanied by a reduction in expenditure. Even if output can rise, it is necessary to ensure that output rises by more than expenditure. In both cases, any impact of a devaluation will be negated by income effects – as in the example in Chapter 6 – unless expenditure is controlled by deflationary policies. Absorption analysis can be used to demonstrate this formally and to put into the appropriate framework statements made at a more elementary level. This is not its sole merit as it is a very flexible framework into which almost any analysis can be put. One of the most common and useful involves the concepts of 'expenditure switching' and 'expenditure reducing'. These would be better named 'output switching' and 'output reducing'. The balance of payments can be improved by either

1. a reduction in expenditure (absorption), without a fall in output (expenditure switching);
2. a reduction in expenditure accompanied by a fall, albeit smaller, in output (expenditure reducing).

Both of these possibilities follow from the basic equation (7.4) above, as do alternatives involving a *higher* level of output, which are usually eliminated from the analysis as impracticable. Policies are usually classified into these two categories by use of analysis based on the elasticities approach. Depreciation, for instance, is classified as expenditure switching. Broadly, a policy is expenditure switching if it would improve the balance of payments if there were no income effects. This, of course, is precisely the question answered by the elasticities model.

In brief then, the absorption approach focuses on the key factors omitted from the traditional approach and provides a general framework of analysis. This can be extended as in the next section, the Mundell model. Precise policy conclusions usually require additional assumptions, as in the fascinating special case of the New Cambridge school (7.4 below). The greatest single virtue of the absorption approach, however, stems from its very existence; the idea that the balance of payments is a macroeconomic variable.

7.2 The Mundell Model

Robert Mundell has been one of the great pioneers of international monetary economics over the last 25 years. The model which bears his name is only one of his many contributions and certainly he no longer thinks it an accurate description of reality, if he ever did. Nevertheless, the Mundell model is important for a number of reasons. One is that UK governments according to its logic from 1951 to 1967. Indeed, one of the reasons for its development was to explore the implications of their actions and those of many other governments who pursued similar policies. Another, more important reason is that it introduces the key concepts of external and internal balance which are central to all advanced Keynesian macroeconomic theory. Moreover, it incorporates the capital account into Keynesian analysis. Finally, the model serves as an introduction to the formal theory of policy making.

The modern theory of economic policy was largely invented by Tinbergen. He showed that a government could achieve as many *targets* as it had instruments available to do it. His whole approach was based on these concepts: that a government manipulates instruments, such as tax rates, so as to achieve targets, such as the level of employment. No government can achieve more targets than it has instruments; this follows from elementary algebra. It is basically the same as the proposition that one can solve n simultaneous equations for n variables. Rather controversially, Tinbergen and his followers went on to argue for *assigning* one instrument to each target. Unfortunately this rule may lead to extreme policies. For example, an assignment rule might be that the budget deficit is increased whenever unemployment is above target and interest rates whenever inflation is above target. As a higher budget deficit would lead to more inflation and higher interest rates to more unemployment, both the budget deficit and interest rates would be raised in order to offset the effect of the other. Tinbergians would argue that so long as the targets were achieved the level of the instruments would not matter, but few others agree. The framework can be extended to incorporate either a cost of changing an instrument or even the notion that a variable can be both a target and an instrument. Nevertheless assignment remains controversial. The relevance of this debate to the present purpose is that the Mundell model implied an optimal assignment and, more important, was drawn up within the Tinbergian target-instrument framework. Many of the more sophisticated models which have followed have continued in this tradition.

Mundell suggested that a government has two instruments: the rate of interest (r) and the level of government spending (G) (or budget deficit). It has two targets: an optimal level of income, the internal target, and a balance of payments target, the external target.

The internal target might be full employment or more generally the level of nominal income which produces the least undesirable combination of unemployment and inflation. Within any conventional macroeconomic framework (e.g. IS-LM) this can be achieved by a large number of combinations of r and G. These combinations are plotted as BB in Figure 7.1, which has interest rates on one axis and G on the other. As, *ceteris paribus*, higher interest rates would reduce income and so require a higher level of G to offset this, BB is upward sloping. Each point along BB represents a combination of policies which will achieve the optimal target level of income. BB is called the internal balance line. As one moves to the right along BB, the increase in G is just enough to offset the increase in r and so keep income at its optimal level. All points to the right of BB imply that a policy has been chosen such that either interest rates are lower or government spending higher than is needed to generate the target level of income. Hence income will be above its target level so there will be excess inflation. Similarly all points to the left of BB imply excess unemployment.

Mundell's model of the balance of payments was in two parts:

1. A model of current account. A higher level of G, or a lower level of r, worsens the current balance because the higher level of income means that more is imported, as in 7.1 above.
2. A model of the capital account. Capital flows are assumed to be interest-sensitive. Thus a higher rate of interest will produce capital inflows.

Governments are assumed to be interested in the sum of these two, a balance of payments definition akin to the balance for official settlements. A higher rate of interest will improve both the current and the capital accounts while a higher level of government spending will worsen the current account. Accordingly, various combinations of r and G will generate the target balance of payments which may be an exact

Figure 7.1: Internal Balance

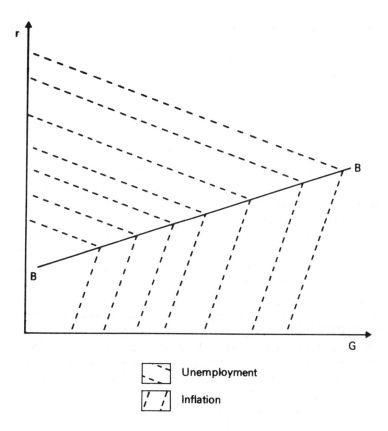

balance or a planned surplus or deficit. These are plotted as FF in Figure 7.2; FF is called the external balance line. Like the internal balance line this is upward sloping – as one moves rightwards along FF, the adverse effect of a higher G is offset by a higher r. A combination of policies represented by a point to the left of FF will produce an excess surplus – since either interest rates are higher or government spending is lower than is necessary for the target (or both). Similarly, any point to the right of FF represents a policy combination which will produce a deficit.

It is necessary to combine Figures 7.1 and 7.2, but to do this one needs to know their relative slopes. FF is the shallower of the two; this follows because interest rates influence balance of payments in two distinct ways. The resulting diagram – Figure 7.3 – shows the outcome

Figure 7.2: External Balance

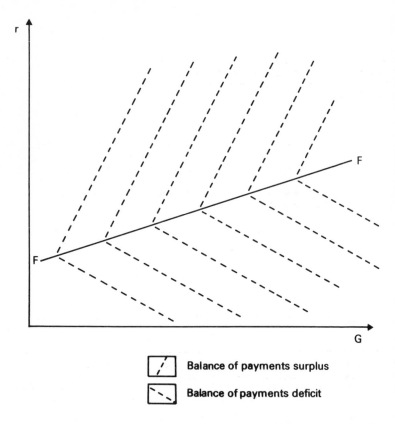

Balance of payments surplus

Balance of payments deficit

of policy options for both external and internal balance; this diagram is often called a Swan diagram after its inventor. The shaded area represents policies which produce an excess surplus and (excess) inflation, etc.

The aim of the Tinbergian approach is to produce crude rules that can be applied in the uncertain real world. The assignment which will work, *so long as BB is steeper than FF*, is:

1. assign G to the internal balance, i.e. increase G if there is excess unemployment and reduce it if there is excess inflation;

2. assign r to the external balance, i.e. reduce r when there is an (excess) surplus and increase it when there is an (excess) deficit.

Figure 7.3: Swan Diagram

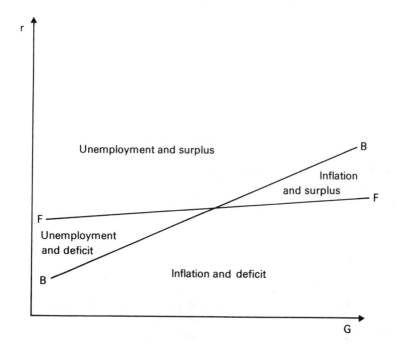

An example of the working of this rule is shown in Figure 7.4. It will also be assumed that the government gives priority to the internal balance. Say the economy starts at (1) with unemployment and a surplus. The government increases G to eliminate unemployment and so (2) is reached where unemployment has been eliminated. The government now reduces r to eliminate the surplus; (3) will therefore be reached. At this point, however, there will be inflation, so G has to be reduced. This process continues but the path is convergent to the optimum. Of course the government could use both tools simultaneously, in which case the path is less tortuous, for example (2A) is reached not (2).

As mentioned above, this policy was used in various countries in the 1950s and 1960s, especially the UK, so it is worth mentioning the defects of the model. The first is that governments are not — and cannot be — indifferent to the capital and current accounts. A £300 million current deficit and a £300 million capital inflow are not the same as a current account balance. If for no other reason the continual

Figure 7.4: Convergence to Equilibrium

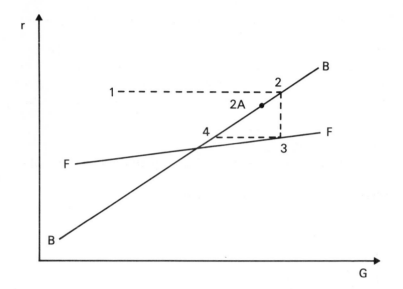

rise in overseas debts — since capital inflows are, after all, borrowing — will mean that interest payments mount and so a new deficit is created. More important, foreign wealth holders will not be prepared to go on lending in such circumstances; they may even withdraw their original loans. Finally, there is a theoretical problem — it should be the *change* in interest rates which induces the inflow not the level. The argument for this postulates stock adjustments by foreign wealth holders. In less high-falutin' language, foreign companies and banks look at interest rates and decide how much to put in each country. If interest rates were, say, 10 per cent in the UK, they might decide their optimal holdings were £15,000 million. If rates are increased to 11 per cent, this might rise to £16,000 million, so there would be an inflow of £1000 million. Unless rates rise again, there would be no further inflow as the foreign holders are already in equilibrium. The UK government learned all this the hard way, by bitter experience in 1965-7.

Besides its historic interest, however, the Mundell model has proved fruitful as a base for more advanced work which has used these key concepts: *external balance; internal balance; assignment*. Whether for good or ill is a moot point. One such development is analysed in the next section: an open economy IS-LM model.

7.3 An Open Economy IS-LM Model

The IS-LM model is usually presented as either a closed economy model or as a pseudo-open economy version. In the latter case 'sterilisation' is assumed, i.e. balance of payments surpluses and deficits are not allowed to influence the money stock, as well as the obvious addition of exports and imports to the withdrawals and injections of the IS curve. As always one can have real income, prices or nominal income on the horizontal axis, in the first two cases price and real income respectively are held constant. It is simplest if prices are held constant, so this will be assumed here.

The first addition to the model is an explicit consideration of the

Figure 7.5: An Open Economy IS-LM Model

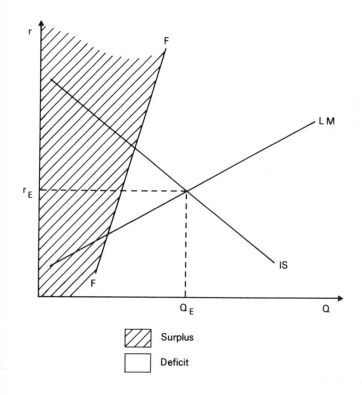

balance of payments. The easiest way to do this is to add an external balance line (FF) to Figure 7.5 representing levels of income and interest rates which generate a balance of payments equilibrium. If one is interested only in the current account it is possible to argue that FF should be vertical − with exogenous exports and fixed price, imports should depend only on income, hence only one level of income will generate equilibrium. Alternatively it could slope backwards − if interest is paid on foreign deposits a higher rate of interest causes a deficit. Usually, however, a Mundell model upward sloping curve for the overall balance is used. Although real income, not government spending, is on the horizontal axis, the same arguments apply, as G influences the balance of payments through Y. Any point to the right of the FF curve represents a deficit (higher income and so more imports) and any point to the left a surplus. Obviously FF could be to the left or right of the equilibrium level of Y and r, Y_E, r_E, i.e. there could be either a surplus or a deficit when the goods and the money markets are otherwise in equilibrium. In Figure 7.5 the initial deficit case is assumed − though as the argument is symmetric the reader can easily work through the alternative of an initial surplus.

The initial deficit reduces the money supply so the LM curve shifts to the left (Figure 7.6). A deficit reduces the money supply in a variety of ways. The simplest are

1. if the government supplies foreign currency to residents to purchase imports, this operates exactly like an open market operation;
2. the ownership of bank deposits may be effectively transferred to foreigners to pay for imports, e.g. if I write a cheque to pay for French wine and the French supplier keeps a deposit with a UK bank. (Foreign-owned deposits are excluded from UK definitions of money.)

The economy will continue with a deficit and a falling money supply until the LM curve has shifted to LM_E at which point, in equilibrium, the level of income has fallen to Y_N, interest rates having risen to r_N and the balance of payments balances.

Alternatively, the government may seek to shift the FF curve, as in Figure 7.7, so that income does not fall. In principle this can be achieved by a devaluation (so long as the modified Marshall-Lerner condition is satisfied). In practice there are problems with the use of the exchange rate, discussed below in Chapters 9 and 10, but in the simple fixed-price case no such problems exist. A depreciation will improve the

Figure 7.6: The LM Curve Shifts

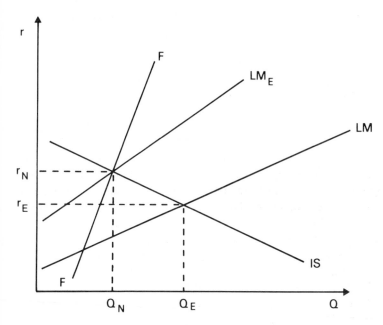

balance of payments at each level of income. Hence it increases the level of income consistent with the balance of payments equilibrium for a given interest rate, i.e. FF shifts rightwards. The authorities have three instruments in this model: money supply, government spending and exchange rate. Thus they can achieve three targets; income, interest rates and balance of payments. Suitable manipulation will make the realisation of any economic goals possible within this model. The real world example is not so amenable, as will be discussed in Chapter 10.

7.4 The New Cambridge School

The New Cambridge School have been exceptionally influential in the UK in that they have almost single-handedly been responsible for the revival of the *macro*-economic case for import controls as a major feature of debates about economic policy. They have to a large extent formulated the economic policies of the 'Tribune' group of the Labour party for almost a decade. The Labour Party's current (1982) official policy. the 'Alternative Economic Strategy', is heavily influenced by

Figure 7.7: Devaluation

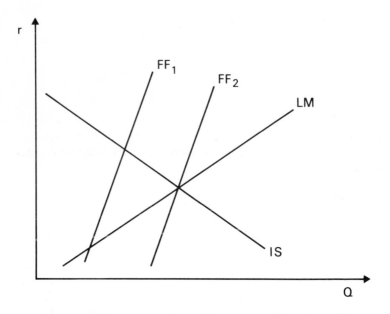

their ideas. In fact the armoury of the New Cambridge economists includes weapons of analysis besides their balance of payments theory. However, none is as well known or as elegant in its derivation of apparent paradoxes from a simple model. Their model seeks to explain the overseas sector's financial surplus. This is the current account plus any purchases of real assets. If a country has a balance of payments deficit on current account of £300 million but non-residents had purchased £100 million of land, antiques (and any other real goods *not* currently produced) from this country, the overseas sector's financial surplus (and the relevant balance of payments deficit) would be £200 million. Transactions in existing real assets are small relative to exports so they will hereafter be ignored, but it is worth noting that X, M, S, T, G and I all have a very slightly different meaning from the standard definition.

As the New Cambridge model is a special case of the absorption approach, it also starts with the national income identity but in this case it is more convenient to use the injections equals withdrawals formulation (in nominal terms):

$$S + T + M = G + X + I$$

Alternatively, a diagrammatic formulation can be used (see appendix). This can be rewritten as

$$(S - I) + (T - G) + (M - X) = 0$$

or as

$$(X - M) = (S - I) + (T - G) \qquad (7.5)$$

The New Cambridge School turns this into a theory of the balance of payments by showing that $(S - I)$ and $(T - G)$ are both determined independently of $(X - M)$ and of each other. Indeed, both are exogenous to this model:

$$(S - I) = k \qquad (7.6)$$

The original version of the model said that $(S - I)$ was a fixed amount, that is the private sector had a fixed *net* level of saving. This would arise in an elementary model if the MPC = 1 and investment were exogenous. In fact, by citing econometric evidence, New Cambridge argued for a marginal propensity to *spend* of one, i.e. if incomes rise by £1 then consumers' expenditure and investment together would rise by £1, e.g. with a MPC of 0.7 and a marginal propensity to invest of 0.3. Later the model was modified to permit credit policy to have an exogenous effect on $(S - I)$. Later still the model was further relaxed but the original assumption still captures the spirit of the model.

$$(T - G) = \bar{F} \qquad (7.7)$$

The economy can be analysed as if the budget deficit $(\bar{F})$, strictly the public sector financial deficit, were exogenous and fixed by the government. This follows from the 'par tax' system. The details do not matter, save to say that both (7.6) and (7.7) are highly controversial. However, if these are accepted, then New Cambridge results follow automatically.

If (7.6) and (7.7) are substituted into (7.4) the crucial result is

$$(M - X) = \bar{F} - k \qquad (7.8)$$

The overseas sector's financial surplus, the balance of payments deficit, is equal to the budget deficit less the constant net saving k. In other words, as F is a policy weapon, by manipulation of F the government can achieve any balance of payments deficit or surplus it wishes. Moreover, this is the only way it, or anybody or anything else, can influence the balance of payments. Hence manipulation of F is both necessary and sufficient to determine (M - X).

Keynesian models basically find two formulae for a variable and then determine the equilibrium level of income (Y_E) as the only value which satisfies both, e.g. to take the simplest case

$$S = I \text{ and } S = 0.1Y$$
$$\text{If} \quad I = 100 \therefore Y_E = 1000$$

The equilibrium level of income is calculated as the only possible level at which saving can equal the exogenous level of investment and 0.1Y simultaneously. The New Cambridge model similarly determines income but uses two formulae for (M - X).

Exports are exogenous to the model, being determined by world trade, relative prices and similar factors. Thus they will be written as $\overline{X}$. New Cambridge have an import function with a unitary income elasticity and a zero price elasticity. Neither are very crucial to the model, although the first simplifies matters as the average propensity to import is equal to the marginal propensity, m. If the price elasticity were unity then the value of imports (M) would be a constant proportion (m) of Y, i.e. M = mY. As the New Cambridge estimate is O however, this means that the *volume of imports* (Q_m) is a constant proportion of the volume of output (Q), i.e.

$$Q_m = mQ$$

To get the value of imports it is necessary to multiply both sides by the price of imports, P_m. Thus

$$M = Q_m P_m = mQP_m \qquad (7.9)$$

It is more convenient to replace Q by $(\frac{Y}{P})$; as Y (nominal income) is equal to Q.P (the price level), hence $Q = \frac{Y}{P}$. Hence (7.9) becomes

$$M = \frac{mYP_m}{P}$$

$(\frac{P_m}{P}$ is the terms of trade and illustrates the impact of changing relative prices on the value of imports.) So,

$$M - X = mYP_{\underline{m}} - \overline{X} \qquad (7.10)$$
$$P$$

(7.10) can be combined with (7.8) to give

$$F - k = mYP_{\underline{m}} - \overline{X}$$
$$P$$

After rearrangement, this gives the equation for the equilibrium level of income:

$$Y = \frac{F - k + \overline{X}}{m} \left(\frac{P}{P_m} \right) \qquad (7.11)$$

This strange-looking equation is in fact the 'multiplier equation' in an unfamiliar guise – the analogue of $\frac{\overline{I}}{MPS}$ in the elementary model. $(F - k + \overline{X})$ is (net) injections. 'm' is the marginal propensity to withdraw. If the import function can be influenced income will alter – but not the level of imports. This is the 'paradox of imports', similar in all respects to the 'paradox of thrift'. Returning to the example used above

$$S = 0.1Y \quad I = 100 \quad Y_E = 1000$$

If people save a higher fraction of their income, income falls but saving is unchanged, at 100, e.g. if the savings propensity doubled

$$S = 0.2Y \quad I = 100 \quad \therefore Y_E = 500$$

This is the traditional paradox of thrift.

Variations in the savings function could be used as a tool of economic policy to influence income. For example if the government could reduce saving to either

$$S = 0.05Y \quad \text{or} \quad S = 0.1Y - 100$$

income would double to 2000 and saving remain at 100.

In an analogous fashion the New Cambridge analysis uses import controls to reduce the level of imports at each level of income. This will increase income but leave the actual total of imports unchanged.

Similarly, devaluation is advocated as a means of improving the balance of payments at each level of income, even though it will not improve the balance of payments since the improvement at each level of income is exactly offset by the imports generated by the higher level of income. The advocacy of the use of exchange rate or import controls to increase income has been a feature of Keynesian analysis since Keynes's *volte face* on the tariff question in 1931. Indeed, the 'foreign trade multiplier' is a standard analytical tool. The New Cambridge contribution is the 'paradox of imports' (and a passionate advocacy of import controls). New Cambridge analysis   presents an apparently bizarre reversal of assignments – the *internal* weapon (the budget deficit) is used to determine the *external* target (balance of payments) and the *external* instrument (import controls) the *internal* target, the level of income (and so employment). This is because import controls influence income but not the balance of payments while the budget deficit influences both income and the balance of payments. By the application of comparative advantage, import controls are used to influence income and the budget deficit the balance of payments. (Just as a doctor who is an expert typist would employ a mediocre typist (with no medical expertise) to type his letters in the elementary textbook example.)

New Cambridge analysis is open to criticism on three counts:

1. the validity of the assumptions concerning (S - I) and (T - G);
2. the danger of retaliation – even though the *level* of imports is unchanged the composition is not, hence foreign governments might take action to reduce UK exports,
3. the long-term damage that protection could do to the UK economy.

In addition, the forecasting record of the New Cambridge school is hotly debated. None of this matters very much for the present purpose. The New Cambridge school provide an interesting example of Keynesian balance of payments analysis and a coherent presentation of the macroeconomic case for import controls and devaluation.

Appendix : A Diagrammatic Presentation of the New Cambridge Model

It is possible to represent the basic results of the New Cambridge school in a number of different ways. An algebraic method was used in the text, p 101 above, and so a diagrammatic method is used here. There are several alternative diagrammatic presentations which can be produced by a modification of one or other of the basic macroeconomic diagrams such as the IS-LM model or the 'Samuelson cross' national income diagram. The method of showing the key results of this school used here is therefore not unique but has the virtue of simplicity. This representation combines the Samuelson cross method of determining rational income with the alternative injections and withdrawals version of the elementary Keynesian model. The basic model is shown in Figure 7.8 (a) of which the upper half of the diagram shows the determination of the equilibrium level of national income (Y_1) where (planned) output is equal to planned expenditure, i.e. where the expenditure function $(C + I + G + X - M)$ intersects the 45 line. The lower half of the diagram shows the level of injections and withdrawals, the equilibrium level of income being where planned injections $(X + I + G)$ equals planned withdrawals $(S + M + T)$. It is, however, more convenient to modify this condition to $M = X + I + G - S - T$. Imports (M) are a function of income so this is shown by the upward sloping line (as the version of the New Cambridge school used here has the MPM = APM at all levels of income, this is a straight line through the origin). The composite $(X + I + G - S - T)$ can be regarded as independent of income so this is horizontal. At the equilibrium level of income (Y_1) imports (M_1) will be equal to $(I + G + X - S - T)$ as shown.

If government spending is increased, this acts as an injection into the system such that income rises. In the upper half of the diagram (Figure 7.8 (b) there is an upward parallel shift of the expenditure function by the amount of the increase in G (in this case ΔJ) such that income rises from Y_1 to Y_2. The same result can be seen in the lower half. $(X + G + I - S - T)$ shifts upwards by ΔJ and at the new equilibrium level of income (Y_2) imports are M_2. $M_2 - M_1$ is necessarily the same as J, since otherwise the equilibrium condition would be violated. Hence imports have risen by exactly the same amount as G. As exports and taxation are unchanged, a rise in the budget deficit $(G - T)$ causes an identical rise in the balance of payments deficit $(M - X)$. The same diagram shows that an exogenous change in exports has no effect on the balance of payments. The rise in exports is also an increase in injections so a rise of ΔJ in exports will cause income to rise from Y_1 to Y_2 and imports from M_1 to M_2. As ΔJ is necessarily equal to $(M_2 - M_1)$, imports and exports rise by the same amount so the balance of payments is unchanged.

In the case of import controls, expenditure on domestically produced goods $(C + I + G + X - M)$ is higher at each level of Y so the expenditure function shifts upwards (the nature of the shift depending

Figure 7.8: The New Cambridge School

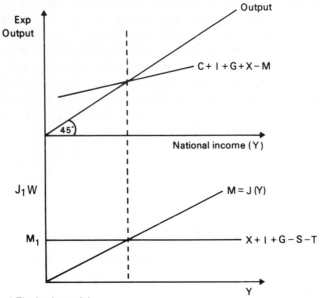

a) The basic model

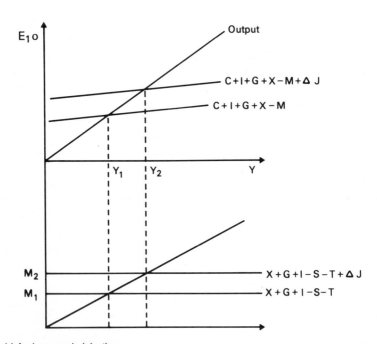

b) An increase in injections

on the form of the control; here both MPM and APM are lower but are still equal to each other). Income rises. In the lower half of the diagram the effect of the controls is to shift the import function, to show that less is imported at each level of income. In equilibrium, imports are still equal to M_1, i.e. to $X + G + I - T - S$. Thus, the balance of payments cannot have improved. A depreciation of sterling would produce both the exogenous change in exports and the shift of the import function, so both analyses would have to be combined but the result would be unchanged − i.e. a higher level of income and an unchanged balance of payments.

8 THE MONETARY THEORY OF THE BALANCE OF PAYMENTS

8.1 Introduction

The monetary theory of the balance of payments, also known as international monetarism, emphasises the financial aspect of the balance of payments, as its name implies. Every transaction is financed in some way or other, usually by the use of money. Hence one might analyse either the financial aspect or the real aspect. Take a primitive tribe whose only transactions with the outside world are the sale of skins for money and the purchase of salt. A balance of payments deficit means that it is receiving a greater value of salt than the skins it is selling. This is the real or goods market aspect of the deficit which is analysed by Keynesian models. Alternatively one might analyse the monetary aspect; it is paying out more money than it is receiving. This is analysed by the monetary theory. A complete analysis must take account of both real and financial factors, so neither Keynesian nor monetary analyses can be complete in themselves. The Keynesian analysis, moreover, is an analysis of *flows* – flows of goods that are traded, and of income. The monetary analysis is an analysis of *stocks*, especially the money stock. Again, as a complete analysis needs to look at both stocks and flows, Keynesian and monetary analyses are complementary as much as competitive. Indeed modern theorists, whether self-styled monetarists or Keynesians, use models which are hybrids of the original international monetarist and Keynesian models. A final preliminary is to note that the monetary theory seeks to explain the overall balance of payments whereas absorption sought to explain the current account. It is possible, therefore, that both are right. This is especially so as the monetary theory puts great emphasis on the capital account – as one of its advocates, Minford, once put it: 'the capital account is King' (when acting as a discussant at the 1978 Money Study Group).

8.2 Domestic and International Monetarism

It is useful to begin an analysis of the monetary theory of the balance of payments by contrasting orthodox and international monetarism.

The latter is an offshoot of the former but nevertheless denies the parent doctrine's main conclusions. This section first presents orthodox monetarist analysis and then shows how the international variant deviates from it.

First of all the behavioural assumption is made that individuals wish to maintain a fixed ratio between

1. their holdings of money (M);
2. their expenditure (or income, at an aggregate level the two are the same), i.e. the price level (P) times the volume of output (Q);
3. their holdings of assets other than money. This is the *value* of asset holdings, i.e. their price of assets (P_a) times the quantity (Q_a), i.e. in symbolic form, the demand for money is such that

$$M \alpha PQ \alpha P_a Q_a$$

If this equilibrium is disturbed individuals and companies will seek to regain it by disposing of (seeking to rebuild) their money holdings. In consequence PQ and $P_a Q_a$ will alter.

For example, suppose the government reduces the quantity of money, the following will ensue:

1. the government reduces the money supply;
2. the private sector is in consequence in disequilibrium because its money holdings are less than demand; so
3. individuals in the private sector seek to rebuild their money balances by
   (a) cutting expenditure, both current and on assets, and
   (b) selling assets.
Firms will behave similarly and may also cut stocks of final output. In consequence
4. there will be excess supply of both goods and assets. By normal microeconomic analysis
5. either the price or the quantity of both goods and assets falls.

Depending on supply elasticities, P may fall and Q remain unchanged or vice versa; more likely both will fall. Similarly either or both P_a and Q_a will adjust, though as some Q_a is fixed (Rembrandts, in theory (!) and land) price adjustments are more likely.

This continues until PQ and $P_a Q_a$ have both fallen by the same amount as the original fall in M.

International monetarism accepts this as far as (4) but then substitute

5a. foreign buyers appear and buy all the excess supply at the previously prevailing price (the small economy assumption). Hence
there is no change in price or output, or the volume or value of
assets. Similarly, if the government increases the quantity of money,
foreigners supply enough goods and assets to meet the consequent
excess demand without price or quantity adjustments.

The foreign purchases (supply) of goods and assets produce a
balance of payments surplus (deficit). This surplus (deficit) necessarily
causes a negative (positive) overseas impact on the money supply such
that the money supply returns to the original level. This story contains
the key feature of the international monetarist story: *a balance of payments surplus or deficit is only temporary because it reflects disequilibrium in the money market.*
An alternative method of analysis looks at the identity

$$\Delta M \equiv DCE \pm 0$$

where 0 is the overseas influence on the money supply. The debate is
about what causal pattern, if any, links these variables. Orthodox
analysis — both Keynes's and Friedman's — argues that DCE and 0
determine M. DCE and 0 may and probably interact. They will do so if,
as both Keynes and Friedman advocate, governments pursue sterilisation operations. However, the key feature of orthodox analysis is that
M is determined by DCE and 0. Moreover, M influences income, either
directly or indirectly, via changes in interest rates. Any impact of DCE
or M on the balance of payments is only via the effect on income and
interest rates. This is set out schematically in Figure 8.1.
The monetary theory of the balance of payments, in stark contrast,
is that 0 adjusts to D and ΔM. ΔM is determined by the demand for
money which is exogenous (as income is invariant), DCE by official
policy. Hence 0 is the variable which adjusts to the difference between
the demand for money and the (domestic) supply of money, DCE is
equal to the change in this domestic supply.
To summarise, in both domestic and international monetarism, the
crucial feature is the demand for money relationship (8.1). However in
domestic orthodox monetarism it is income which adjusts to ensure the
equality of the demand for and supply of money. In international
monetarism, it is the balance of payments. Thus, the fundamental

Figure 8.1: Orthodox and International Monetarist Analysis

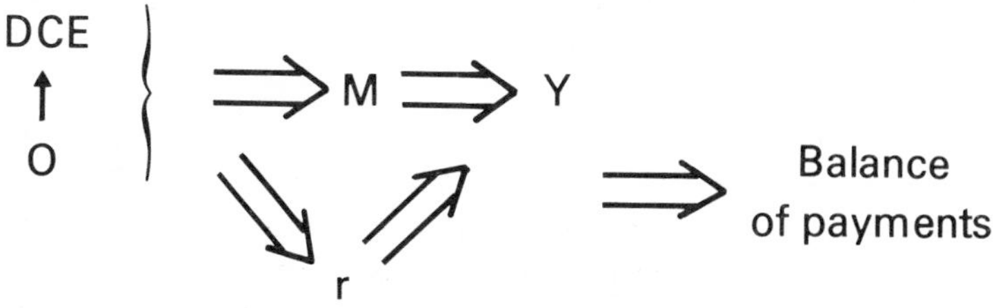

DCE }
↑   } ⟹ M ⟹ Y
O   }   ↘   ↗   ⟹ Balance
              r   of payments

The orthodox model

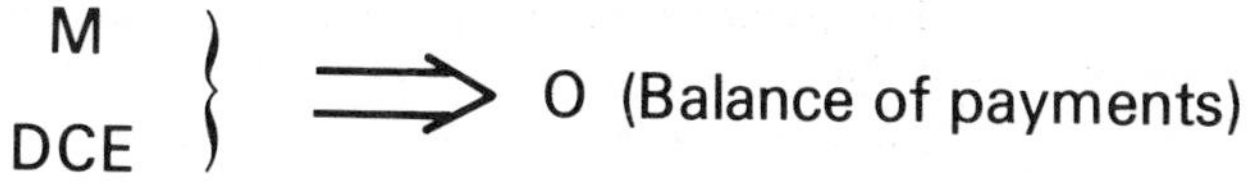

M   }
DCE } ⟹ O (Balance of payments)

International monetarism

monetarist proposition of a direct link between money and nominal
income disappears.

8.3 The Exchange Rate and the Analysis of the Balance of Payments

The foregoing analysis presented the essence of the monetary theory of
the balance of payments as a temporary feature of stock disequilibrium
in the money market. In this section this analysis will be extended to
incorporate the exchange rate and to produce a modified model more
relevant to large and medium-sized economies.

In section 8.2 the exchange rate was effectively fixed. This followed
from the assumption that foreigners would buy all assets at prevailing
prices. This included assets denominated in domestic currency; in the
simplest case, non-resident demand for pound notes was perfectly
elastic at, say, \$1.75. This assumption will now be relaxed. Instead
non-residents will be assumed to have a perfectly elastic demand for
UK real assets and goods at a price *in dollars*. However, their demand
for financial assets, denominated in sterling, will depend on the
exchange rate. This assumption is more plausible than the one used in
section 8.2 and so is used by most international monetarists, 'almost

invariably' as the founding father put it (Johnson, p. 153, of Frenkel and Johnson).

In this case some slight modifications have to be introduced into the story above. The new story continues:

5b. The excess supply of goods and real assets is still purchased by foreigners but non-residents do not purchase all the financial assets offered. In consequence the exchange rate falls.

6. The fall in the exchange rate leads to a rise in domestic prices.

7. The real value of the money supply falls (alternatively because P and P_a have risen the demand for money rises). So, as the *nominal* quantity of money need not fall to the original level, merely the *real* level, the equilibriation of money supply and demand is achieved in part by a rise in price as well as by a balance of payments deficit (and a fall in price as well as a surplus for an initial reduction in the money supply).

This analysis can be illustrated by Figure 8.2. The domestic producers of a good are necessarily price takers because it is a small

Figure 8.2: A Change in the Exchange Rate

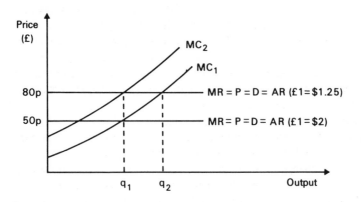

economy. Hence, the domestic producers of widgets face a horizontal marginal revenue curve. This will be at the world price divided by the exchange rate. If the exchange rate is $2 = £1 and the world price of widgets is $1, the world price of a widget, expressed in sterling, is 50p

($1 ÷ 2). The UK producers can sell as much as they like at 50p but not at any higher price, because they are 'small'. Hence, they face a horizontal marginal revenue curve at 50p. Hence, in Figure 8.2, with marginal cost curve mc_1 a typical firm's output will be q_1. When the exchange rate changes, the marginal revenue curve will shift. If the exchange rate falls to $1.25, the new world price of a widget, expressed in sterling, will be 80p, i.e. the world price in dollars divided by the exchange rate ($1 ÷ 1.25$). Thus the firm will face a new higher marginal revenue curve, at 80p. The new equilibrium output is q_2 and the equilibrium price is 80p. However, all costs including wages will rise by the same amount so ultimately the marginal cost curve will shift from mc_1 to mc_2 and output will fall to q_1. The analysis of the cost curve shift is considered in detail on p. 142 below. Here all that is relevant is that it is optimal for every firm to raise its prices so monetary expansion raises the price level through its effect on the exchange rate.

This result is closer to orthodox monetarism in that a rise in the money supply does lead to a rise in prices. However, the mechanism is different and there is no proportional (or even fixed) relationship between money and nominal income or prices. The validity of international monetarism depends on the validity of the premise that foreign purchases/supply will always equilibriate both goods and asset markets at the previously prevailing dollar price. This is necessarily true for a small economy — indeed it defines a small economy as in the microeconomic analysis of tariffs (p. 41 above). It is equally necessarily wrong for a large economy. Hence the theory is applicable to Luxemburg but not to the USA. The problem is that most economies are neither large nor small; Germany, the UK, Australia, Japan are all medium-sized. Perhaps the best solution is to treat such countries as facing an elastic but not horizontal supply curve in which international monetarism is relevant as a polar case.

Further complexities can be introduced to analyse medium-sized economies. One is that the change in the exchange rate may induce shifts between real and financial assets. The effect is likely to be to reduce the effects of a change in the money supply. The other is that there may be short-term effects from the change in exchange rate, i.e. the rise in output from q_1 to q_2 in Figure 8.2. Some analysts feel that this has been important in the UK in 1980-81 when, it is argued, a rising exchange rate caused unemployment.

In this modified form, the international monetarist doctrine is still that a balance of payments surplus or deficit is a temporary phenomenon caused by money market disequilibrium. The addition is that disequilibrium will also influence exchange rates and so prices (and possibly employment in the short term). The influence of the exchange rate on the economy is discussed further in Chapter 10. However, the international monetarist message is clear. Monetary policy will have a direct effect on the balance of payments and on the exchange rate. The impact, if any, of monetary policy on prices and output will be through this channel. These propositions have been very influential in the last ten years, although the consensus position would be 'a major effect of monetary policy is through the exchange rate' rather than 'the only . . .'.

Most international monetarists, e.g. one of the founding fathers, Dornbusch (e.g. 1980), are prepared to accept much more substantial modifications of the simplistic model. Notably income need not be exogenous, as in 8.2, nor need everyone be a price taker, as above. The balance of payments will still be the difference between the domestic supply (DCE) and demand for money. However, both DCE and the demand for money, as well as income and interest rates, are all endogenous. One way of analysing such models is:

$$0 = \Delta \text{ Demand for money} - DCE \qquad (8.1)$$

(a positive 0 implying a surplus on the balance of payments)
The change in the demand for money can be replaced by the demand for money function, i.e. the changes in wealth (W), output (Q), prices (P) and interest rates (r) which change the demand for money. Thus (8.1) becomes (using a linear demand for money relationship)

$$0 = \Delta (a + bW + cQ + dP - er) - DCE \qquad (8.2)$$

DCE can be replaced by its definition: PSBR + Δ bank lending Y (ΔBLP) - Δ private lending to public sector (ΔPLG) and to the non-bank private sector, and the first part rewritten to give

$$0 = b\Delta W + c\Delta Q + d\Delta P - e\Delta r - (PSBR + \Delta BLP - \Delta PLG)$$

or

$$0 = b\Delta W + c\Delta Q + d\Delta P - e\Delta r - PSBR - \Delta BLP + \Delta PLG \qquad (8.3)$$

(8.3) can be used to analyse the impact of anything on the balance of payments, e.g. public spending, taxation and interest rates, and the result simply compared to the absorption approach. Some changes are very simple in their effect. An exogenous change in wealth (e.g. the discovery of oil in the North Sea) improves the balance of payments as wealth holders have a higher demand for money which the overseas sector satisfies. An exogenous change in income (e.g. when the oil is brought ashore) similarly improves the balance of payments by affecting the demand for money (and in no other way). This highlights a critical difference between the absorption and monetary approaches. In the Keynesian approach an exogenous increase in income will worsen the balance of payments, unless caused by an increase in exports. The monetary approach says it will improve it, irrespective of cause. Thus, for example, a shift in the consumption function or marginal efficiency of capital schedule (or an induced increase in house-building that does not involve extra government spending of lower interest rates) will improve the balance of payments for an international monetarist and worsen the current account for a Keynesian. For the Keynesian the argument is simple; a higher level of income will raise the level of imports. For the international monetarist, a higher level of income increases the demand for money and so causes a temporary disequilibrium in the money market. Demand for money is less than supply so the private sector rebuilds its money balances by sales of goods and assets to the overseas sector, i.e. by a balance of payments surplus. McCloskey and Zecher, in Frenkel and Johnson (1976), p. 368, highlight this difference and try to show that the empirical validity of the monetary theory is thereby demonstrated for the gold standard period, when rises in income seem to have been followed by improvements in the balance of payments (gold inflows). Some changes are rather more complex in that they may increase both the demand for and supply of money. For example, an increase in public spending in a recession would increase the PSBR and (DCE) and so worsen the balance of payments by increasing the supply of money, but this would partly be offset by the higher demand generated by the higher level of income. In many cases, the analysis yields ambiguous results unless special assumptions are made.

To conclude the monetary theory of the balance of payments has enriched balance of payments theory by

1. Stressing the importance of stocks in balance of payments theory.
2. Emphasising the monetary counterpart to a balance of payments surplus or deficit and the consequent need for explicit analysis of the demand for and the supply of money.

3. Emphasising the role of the exchange rate as a transmission mechanism for monetary policy (see Chapter 10) and the likelihood of direct links between monetary policy and the balance of payments.

8.4 Devaluation and the Monetary Approach

Depreciation of the currency, or the policy weapon of devaluation, influences the balance of payments in the monetary approach only in so far as it effects either the demand for money or DCE, the change in the domestic money supply. This effect in principle could go either way and in general is likely to be small.

The simplest monetary approach to devaluation is, using the model presented in 8.2: the rise in the domestic price level reduces the *real* value of money holdings. There is a consequent reduction in expenditure and sale of assets both because of (Pigou) wealth effects and to reattain equilibrium by rebuilding money balances. In consequence there is a balance of payments surplus in the short-term. Kuska (e.g. 1972) was the first to make this aspect of the theory clear but Johnson popularised it and summarised is as follows: 'devaluation is equivalent to domestic credit contraction; its function is to deflate domestic real balances and thereby to cause domestic residents to attempt to restore their real balances through the international commodity and security markets' (in Frenkel and Johnson (1976), p. 165). It is interesting that this involves the opposite requirement to the traditional approach wherein domestic inflation reduces the effectiveness of a devaluation, here it is essential.

This 'beneficial transitory effect on reserves and the balance of payments' (Johnson, a few pages later) 'can be offset or neutralized by a variety of factors, such as the rise in interest rates which may also be caused by devaluation'. DCE itself may be affected by the devaluation, for example, if government expenditure is maintained in real terms the PSBR may rise. Obviously the PSBR could fall if higher prices increase tax yields. The flow demand for public sector debt is likely to fall at least in the short term. The demand for credit may rise; it almost certainly will to finance increased (nominal) stocks. In general, depreciation sets off many mechanisms and so the outcome is complex and depends upon how domestic monetary policy operates. There is no clear definition of a neutral policy and so one cannot say, *a priori*, what the *ceteris paribus* effects of devaluation are on DCE.

8.5 The Determination of the Exchange Rate

One of the features of the modified international monetarist model presented in 8.2 was that the exchange rate was endogenous, whereas in both Chapters 6 and 7 it was exogenous. Of course, the rate is endogenous in the sense that rate is determined within the foreign exchange market but official intervention can and does occur in this market such that exogenity may not be an unreasonable assumption (as with interest rates). The foreign exchange market is analysed in Chapter 9 and official intervention in Chapter 11. However, it is useful at this point to list the market forces which might influence the exchange rate, or determine the cost of official intervention. In any securities market, the basic forces determining supply and demand are rates of return and expected price change but the schedules may be shifted by exogenous economic factors. Moreover expectations are likely to be influenced by economic theories and variables. The economic factors are:

1. *interest rates*, because they are an influence on the rate of return on investments in one currency rather than another;
2. *domestic credit expansion*, following international monetarist analysis;
3. *relative prices* (i.e. inflation compared to the world level), either directly (purchasing power parity theory) or because of the influence on the balance of payments (traditional theory);
4. *government spending* (or the PSBR) as the determinant of the balance of payments on current account within the Keynesian models;
5. *the trade balance or current account balance* because they affect the supply and demand for currencies directly and a change in the exchange rate might be needed to induce the offsetting effect on the other parts of the balance of payments.

9 THE FOREIGN EXCHANGE MARKET

9.1 Some Concepts

The foreign exchange market is a market in which currencies are bought and sold; many people use it to obtain currency for a holiday. Thus francs are traded for pounds and pounds for dollars and so on. The price of one currency in terms of another is called the *exchange rate*.[1] If one currency is traded against two others, there is an implied exchange rate between the latter, called the *cross rate*. If the pound is traded for two dollars and a dollar for two Deutschmarks, this implies a cross rate of four DM to the pound. If this cross rate differed from the actual sterling-DM rate, then *arbitrageurs* would intervene to profit by the discrepancy and, of course, in the process remove it. The market in currency for immediate delivery is called the *spot* market. There are also *forward* markets in which an agreement is made to exchange currency at a specified price on a particular date, both price and date being fixed when the agreement is made, irrespective of any future fluctuations in exchange rates. Forward markets, discussed below in sections 9.2 and 9.4, are of great value to both traders and speculators (see also p. 182). A *speculator* is a person who hopes to make a profit by correctly predicting a change in exchange rates. If the forward rate is £1=$1.70 for delivery in three months' time and the speculator expects the rate then to be $1.50, he can sell forward sterling. He commits himself to delivering, say, £100,000 in three months' time, knowing that he will receive $170,000 in exchange. If he is right about the exchange rate, he will be able to buy the £100,000 in the spot market for $150,000 and so make $20,000 profit. If he is wrong, he might make a very large loss.

Traders are only involved in the market as a necessary consequence of their other activities, e.g. an exporter or a holiday-maker. Because they need to transact with residents of other countries they need to obtain foreign currency or to dispose of it to meet obligations in the UK. These traders can insure themselves by a suitable forward contract. Imagine a student who has planned a holiday in the US in September which will cost her $1000. She intends to work in July and August to finance this holiday but will be paid in sterling. She does not know how much she needs to earn to pay for the holiday unless she uses the forward market. If the rate were $2.50, £400 would be enough; if it were $1.50, £600 would be needed — and both rates have been seen recently. Hence the student does not know how much work she needs to do. If, however, she buys $1000 forward at say $2=£1, she commits herself to delivering £500 on 1 September knowing she will receive the $1000 in exchange. Hence she knows how many hours of dishwashing she needs to do to ensure her holiday. This transaction is often called 'hedging'; the student has hedged what would otherwise be her bet on the exchange rate.

Economic analysis of the foreign exchange market makes extensive use of these three categories — the trader, the speculator and the *arbitrageur* — who take certain profits and, in doing so, reduce market irregularities. However, in the real world the same agents often engage in all three. Moreover it is often impossible to decide into which category a transaction falls, even with complete knowledge of the agent's position. A failure to hedge might be viewed as speculation; if one normally hedges it is, since behaviour has been changed in the hope of profiting from a change in exchange rates. If Ford of Detroit sell pounds forward, are they protecting themselves against a fall in the dollar value of their sterling asset (Ford of Dagenham) or speculating? The categorisation of foreign exchange transactions has often proved fruitful but it can be carried too far. In the last resort, every dealer is a utility maximiser and, usually, a profit maximiser; further description is superrogatory.

Governments have usually intervened in foreign exchange markets to influence the exchange rate. The methods of doing this are discussed below, p.152, but the arguments for and against intervention are discussed in this chapter. This debate has usually taken the form of a discussion of the case for fixed and floating rates. The problem with this is that there are many varieties of each and many of the arguments used in the debate only apply to a particular exchange rate regime, not to floating rates or to fixed rates generally.

The usual definition of a *floating rate* system is that it is one without the (fixed) par value that characterises a *fixed rate* regime. The *par* value of a currency is the rate at which the authorities in a country have committed themselves to buy and sell their currency. The best examples of this are the gold standard and the Bretton Woods system. However their differences are greater than their similarities. The gold standard was really only effective between the UK and the US. Both countries were committed to maintaining a rate of $4.88665=£1; strictly both committed themselves to buying and selling their own currency for gold at a fixed price but these prices implied an exchange rate. The exchange fluctuated a little around the parity, between the so-called gold points, because it was not profitable to sell dollars for gold, ship the gold across the Atlantic and buy. pounds or vice versa unless the deviation from the parity were large enough to cover shipping, insurance and interest rate costs. (The latter arose because no interest was earned on the gold while it crossed the Atlantic.) Bretton Woods was an attempt to imitate this system by an agreement that each country would declare a par value against the dollar and keep the actual rate within 1 per cent of this. However, the par value could be changed by the government of the country and hence the system produced very little of the stability of the gold standard. At least, after 1896, there was no speculation under the gold standard (and very little intervention) as the rate was genuinely fixed, hence there was no conceivable gain from speculation. Under Bretton Woods, there was massive speculation, effectively betting on a change of par value (see p. 128 below).

Thus it is necessary to define exchange rate regimes carefully and to be equally careful in ensuring that the arguments for and against them are really applicable to the regime being considered.

Free floating is a system in which the authorities never intervene (and in which no one expects them to intervene). This is unknown; the nearest example is the Austro-Hungarian-Russian exchange rate between 1889-1914, although even here there was some indirect intervention, e.g. via the famous Russian Bear Squeeze of 1891 on the rouble-franc rate.

'Dirty floating' is a system in which the rate is managed by the authorities without a par value. Hence the rate is under official influence but the authorities are not committed to any particular form or amount of intervention. Examples include the sterling-dollar rate from 1931-9, August-December 1971 and since June 1972. Obviously there may be very heavy or very light intervention. The authorities may virtually peg the rate or allow it almost total freedom. This is usually described in terms of the cleanness of the float; very dirty floating or a fairly clean float would describe the two situations above. Linguistic purists would rightly say that these terms both mix metaphors and overstrain them, but the terms seem to have stuck.

A *fully fixed* exchange rate regime is one in which the rate:

1. has a par value;
2. this parity is fixed forever;
3. participants in the market believe it to be fixed forever.

The closest to this is the sterling-dollar rate from 1876 (the crime of '76) to 1914, the gold standard era, but for most of this period maintenance of the gold standard was a major US political issue. In 1893-4 it appeared that the US might be forced off it by heavy speculation; eventually a loan on usurious terms from the Morgan Bank enabled the US to maintain the parity. In 1896 and 1900, the breaking of the link with gold and sterling was the major campaign plank of Bryan, the Democratic presidential candidate, who did not want to 'crucify mankind on a cross of gold'. Hence (3) was certainly not true until 1896 and (2) was in doubt. (There was also a group of countries, the Latin Monetary Union, partly on the gold standard, the so-called Limping gold standard.)

The rarity of free floating and fully fixed exchange rates needs to be stressed because of the fact that many arguments apply to these extremes and not elsewhere. 'Discipline', 'certainty' and the absence of speculation are all advantages of fully fixed but not of *semi fixed* exchange rate regimes, e.g. adjustable parity schemes. The best known of these was Bretton Woods, see above. The gold exchange standard, 1925-31, was very similar.

There are also systems in which the par value is adjusted from day to day, e.g. the *crawling peg*, used by Brazil from 1967. In this the parity was a weighted, moving average of past actual values. 'Wide bands' was a strange scheme, apparently designed to combine the worst of both dirty floating and Bretton Woods by having par values but 10 per cent fluctuation on either side (see p.167 below).

Finally, in terminology, the EEC has sought to produce a variety of schemes to link its members' currencies in an (adjustable parity) semi-fixed scheme: the European Monetary Union (1972-5) and European Monetary System (1979-). These and their partial failure have produced a menagerie of groupings − including snake (all nine), mini-snake (or DM bloc) (Germany, Holland, Sweden, Denmark, Austria (sometimes) and Belgium), worm (Benelux), mini-worm (Belgium and Luxemburg). It is not clear who gains by such a proliferation of jargon except financial journalists anxious to show off and publishers of dictionaries of financial slang.

9.2 The Interest Parity Theory

The interest parity theory was first promulgated by Keynes in 1923 (Keynes, 1923). It is a theory concerning the relationship amongst four variables: the spot exchange rate, the forward rate, the domestic interest rate and the foreign rate. It is extensively used for a variety of purposes, see for example Sohmen's argument below and the final paragraph of this section.

The theory is one of arbitrage, i.e. it argues that if investors are offered a costless, riskless profit they will take it. The consequence will be the ultimate elimination of the opportunity, since one or other price will adjust in response to the investors' activity. If good x is on sale in town A at 20p and town B at 30p and it costs 5p to ship the good between A and B, *arbitrageurs* can profit by buying in A and selling in B. The increased demand in A will tend to drive price up and the increased supply in B to reduce price until the gap is 5p. (A final possibility is that the increased demand for transport facilities raises the transport cost but the equilibrium differential is the transport cost.)

The interest arbitrage calculation is as follows where:

R^N = the New York interest rate paid on deposits or loans in dollars

R^L = the London interest rate paid on deposits or loans in sterling

F = the forward exchange rate

S = the spot exchange rate

(F and S are both expressed as dollars per pound.)

Initially it is assumed:

S = \$2 F = \$1.96 (for one year ahead)

R^N = 10 per cent p.a. R^L = 12 per cent p.a.

If \$1000 is invested in New York, the return is \$1100 in one year's time. Alternatively, the \$1000 can be converted into £500 and invested in London, in which case the return will be £560 in one year's time. It is not clear whether £560 or \$1100 will be more attractive in one year's time, but the investor can *cover* himself by a forward transaction. He can sell £560 forward and guarantee himself a return of \$1108 = 80 (560 times the forward rate of \$1.96). Hence it is preferable to invest dollars indirectly by the triple transaction of a spot transaction, a sterling deposit and a forward sale than directly. Hence investors will do this. If the rate were \$1.90, the return would be \$1064, so the dollar deposit would be preferred.

Someone wishing to invest, say, £1000 in sterling faces a similar choice. He can invest directly in sterling and receive \$1120 in a year's time or convert the sterling into dollars (\$2000), deposit them (to receive \$2200) and cover himself by selling forward the resulting dollar return, to receive £1111.11. With the rates as set out above, he would prefer a direct deposit. However, if the forward rate were $1.90, the indirect deposit would accrue to £1162.63 and would be preferred to the direct deposit.

Substituting general for specific values, the return on the indirect deposit is $\dfrac{S(1 + R^N)}{F}$ The rate of return on indirect deposits can be calculated for any period — e.g. one day, one month, three months — as well as for the hypothetical year used in the examples above. An investor considering a sterling deposit will compare R^L with $\dfrac{S(1 + R^N)}{F}$

and invest accordingly, in either a direct or an indirect deposit.

The gap between the two returns is called the *covered differential* and is a major determinant of capital flow; when it is positive, funds flow into London and vice versa. Some investors might compare the *uncovered returns* (R^L and R^N) but most will look at the covered differential, because they would otherwise bear an unnecessary risk.

The equilibrium condition is that the two covered returns are equal and the covered differential is equal to zero, i.e.

$$R^L = \frac{S(1 + R^N)}{F} \qquad (9.1)$$

This can be generalised to any pair of currencies and any foreign and domestic interest rate, in which case the condition for equilibrium is

$$R_H = \frac{S(1 + R_F)}{F} \qquad (9.2)$$

where R_H = the domestic and R_F the foreign interest rate.

It is useful sometimes to set out the equilibrium difference between the rates in which case (9.2) can be transformed into

$$R_H - R_F = S - \frac{F - S}{S} \qquad (9.3)$$

$\dfrac{F - S}{S}$ is the difference between spot and forward rates expressed as a percentage of the spot rate. $\dfrac{F - S}{S}$ is called the *forward premium* (and $\dfrac{S - F}{S}$ the *forward discount*). When there is a forward premium the forward rate exceeds the spot rate and vice versa. The theory is sometimes stated in terms of the forward discount and premium, e.g. that R_H should equal R_F plus the forward discount or R_F less the forward premium.

Keynes went on to argue that the equilibrium condition would be satisfied because the volume of arbitrage funds would be infinite. If the covered differential were not zero, either all investors would prefer an indirect to a direct sterling deposit if $RL < \dfrac{S(1+RN)}{F}$, or all would prefer an indirect to direct dollar deposit, if $RL > \dfrac{S(1+RN)}{F}$. However, in addition to these there could be a large quantity of pure arbitrage transactions. Returning to the original example (with S = $2, F = $1.96, RN = 10 per cent and RL = 12 per cent) the investor could invest $1000 and receive $100 interest, or convert (to £500), lend in sterling (and guarantee £500) and sell £560 forward to guarantee a return of $1108 = 80 which would give him $108 = 80 interest. However, the investor could alternatively borrow $1000 and incur an obligation to repay together with $100 interest. He could then convert, lend sterling and sell forward to guarantee the same return as before. The $1108 = 80 would enable him to repay the loan and the interest and have a return of $8.80 on an investment of zero. Indeed, he has every incentive to do this, since it is a riskless, costless profit. In fact, he might as well borrow $1 million and multiply his profit. In principle there will an infinite quantity of arbitrage transactions so long as the forward rate were $1.96. If the forward rate were $1.90, then there would be a similar incentive to borrow pounds, convert and buy sterling forward. If an *arbitrageur* borrowed £1000, he would have to repay £1120. His £1000 would be converted into $2000. Thus he would be able to invest it to obtain $2200 in one year's time. If he sold at £1.90, this would guarantee a return of £1157.88. Hence he would clear £37 = 88p on an investment of zero. Again, with an infinite return there is an incentive to operate on an infinite scale.

In theory there should therefore be an infinite quantity of arbitrage to ensure that Keynes's interest parity theory is satisfied. In practice there always used to be a large, but variable margin such that a purchase of sterling matched by a forward sale always offered a better return than a dollar investment. It was always puzzling why this was so (see Gowland (1979), p. 61), especially after the growth of Eurocurrency market, since the theory held in these markets. This often created a margin of 2 or 3 per cent in favour of an investment in Euro- rather than domestic sterling. This was still more puzzling since the deposit was with a different branch of the same bank. Exchange control, in principle, could not explain the observation since it did not apply to external holders of sterling, some of whom neither arbitraged Keynes-style nor even switched funds from Lloyds of London to Lloyds of Paris. However, as the differential virtually disappeared after the abolition of UK exchange control in November 1979, the paradox presumably stemmed from this.

The theory, that $R^F - R^H = S + \dfrac{F - S}{S}$, is used to explain any of the interest rates, spot rates and forward rates by different economists since, of course, if any three are given, the fourth follows *a fortiori*. Some economists have argued that domestic interest rates are fixed in this way, using a 'small country' assumption. R^F is the world level of rates, S and F being market or exogenously fixed so the domestic authorities have no choice but to accept the implied level of domestic interest rates; they are too small to influence world rates. Other theories explain why interest rates influence exchange rates, and how governments can use interest rates to influence them (see p. 156 below). Keynes himself argued that a government willing to fix the forward premium (discount) at the appropriate level could then have both the exchange rate and the interest rate of its choice. No one denies that a government could fix either, but Keynes argued that the forward rate could be an extra instrument and so ensure the fulfilment of an extra target. Finally the theory can be used to derive the forward rate or to show the profitability of offering forward cover. This is Sohmen's argument, p. 131 below.

9.3 Fixed and Floating Rates

The remainder of this chapter is devoted to an analysis of the arguments used for and against different regimes of exchange rate management. It is remarkable how many of the arguments start with an *a priori* assumption that governments are necessarily incompetent. However, some deduce from this that they should be constrained by fixed rate, others that they should be denied any power to influence exchange rates, let alone to determine them; Rueff (1967) and Friedman (1953) being the leading advocates of these two views. This is typical of much of the analysis in two ways. On the one hand, a lot of the argument is politico-economic rather than narrowly economic-theoretic. Obviously it is not necessarily the worse for this, indeed 'political economy' is the only satisfactory way to approach exchange rates but it contributes to the second feature of the literature, the number of two-edged arguments used.

The oldest argument for fully fixed rates is the need for *'discipline'*. Rueff used to be the leading advocate of this (e.g. 1967) but it is now mainly used by the American liberal 'New Right', e.g. Brennan and Buchanan (1975). The argument is that governments are naturally prone to overspend and so create inflation. *With fully fixed exchange rates, governments cannot inflate.* At worst the budget deficit leads to a balance of payments deficit whose absorptive and monetary effect is to avert the inflation. In a closed economy a government can create inflation either by increasing demand for goods relative to supply (Keynesian analysis), in which case, as an open economy, the deficit means that foreign supply (imports) exceeds foreign demand (exports) so the inflationary outcome is avoided; or, alternatively, government spending is financed by money creation which is inflationary (monetarist analysis). In this case, the balance of payments deficit leads to a countervailing fall in the money supply through a negative overseas impact. At best the need to maintain the fixed rate prevents the government from spending. At worst the inflationary effect is averted by a system of fully fixed exchange rates. There are a number of problems with this argument. To seek to constrain a government is normally regarded as an anti-democratic attitude in the UK and by many US commentators. Buchanan *et al.* however, would argue that it is democratic to constrain a government because in this way the electors' wishes prevail against those of utility-maximising bureaucrats. Buchanan would argue that any written constitution constrains a government and that he merely wants to add an economic constraint to the political constraints of the US Constitution, especially the Bill of Rights. Perhaps to quote the old text book cliché, the US Constitution is Republican but not Democratic, but that it is eminently reasonable to be undemocratic about such matters as freedom from arbitrary arrest. Whether freedom from inflation should be similarly sacred is a complex question of political theory which is beyond the scope of this book. However, even if the *'discipline'* argument is acceptable on philosophic grounds, the argument can be stood on its head by the *autonomy* argument. This is that a government needs a floating rate to permit it to manage its economy. This is sometimes put as the argument that governments should be able to inflate if they want to, or, more optimistically, have the power to avoid unemployment. Equally often, however, the argument comes from hard-line monetarists (e.g. Friedman (1953) and Friedman and Roosa (1961)). They argue that governments need to be able to determine the money supply so as to keep it either constant or growing at 2 per cent p.a. This power is denied to governments under fully fixed rates. The Rueff-Buchanan school are ready to accept an exogenous rate of inflation, determined by gold production or other countries' actions, since rigid exchange rates constrain everyone to the world average. Friedman wants to aim at price stability. Hence the hard-nosed Right can agree on their analysis but not the conclusion. It can never be clear whether a rigid exchange rate or a monetary rule is preferable, as, for example, Buchanan admits.

More seriously still, once one leaves the world of fully fixed rates, the arguments are no longer clear-cut. This affects those anxious to equip governments with the power to manage economies just as much as those anxious to constrain them. Once there is the opportunity of changing the parity, discipline can be evaded. Furthermore, there is no way that a government can be forced to keep for ever the rigid system — it can always break away, although constitutional provisions may restrict it, or simply not support the exchange rate and leave its opponents to work out how to force it to obey the law. Overseas factors influence governments in various ways:

1. their pure economic effect — e.g. the effect of the exchange rate on inflation;
2. through the need to obey the rules of the game of the international monetary system;
3. through the electorate's reaction to, say, a change in the exchange rate.

One can find examples of when a semi-fixed system has constrained a government through those mechanisms; the best known is the UK in 1964-7 (see Beckerman (1972)). Equally, however, overseas factors constrained the Labour government in 1975-6, albeit in a different way under dirty floating. The Heath government evaded all constraints under both semi-fixed parities and dirty floating to expand the money supply by 60 per cent in 27 months, the era of 'Barberism'. (For all the above, see Gowland (1982a) and references therein.)

In summary, 'discipline' and 'autonomy' depend much more upon the workings of the political system and upon personalities than upon exchange rate regimes, e.g. Germany has had very low and Italy high inflation since 1948, irrespective of the exchange rate regime.

One argument can be dismissed immediately; this is the argument that freely floating exchange rates will ensure that the *balance of payments is self-righting*. The analysis in Chapters 6 to 8 showed that depreciation may not eliminate a (current account) deficit or vice versa, largely because of income effects. The balance of payments is a macro-economic variable and so cannot be influenced solely by microeconomic means. This point, like all the analysis in Chapters 6 to 8, emphasises the strongest argument for some official intervention in the foreign exchange market which is that *the exchange rate has such an effect upon the economy, especially upon inflation and unemployment, that no government can renounce intervention.* Even Friedman agrees that withdrawal from the foreign exchange market should be the capstone of a *laissez-faire* policy, not the initiation of it (in his debate with Roosa, 1967). The scope for, and role of, exchange rate policy is further considered in Chapter 10.

If it were accepted that some intervention is necessary, it would still be necessary to consider what form of regime is best. Ruling out the fully fixed system, one has to choose between dirty floating and adjustable parities. Two arguments are relevant: one in favour of and the other against dirty floating. The argument for dirty floating is that, because of *one-way options*, it is impossible to maintain even a temporary, fixed parity (or at least prohibitively expensive). The problem arises because, with adjustable parities, there are usually only the possibilities that an exchange rate will remain unchanged or move in one known direction, i.e. a symmetric distribution is impossible. Throughout the 1960s it was clear that the UK would never change its parity upwards, nor Germany downwards: there was only a one-way option. Hence most of the risk of speculation disappeared. The sterling exchange rate was $2.79 in September 1967 and a calculation could be made of the losses from speculation if the rate were to remain unchanged and this be compared with the likely gain if there were a devaluation. This ratio could then be compared with the (subjective) probability of devaluation. There was no risk of (upward) revaluation so the speculation was attractive. For example, in September 1967, the authorities were effectively offering odds of 5-1 against a devaluation within three months. Understandably, this proved so very attractive that when the bet won (in November 1967) the UK taxpayers had to bear the very heavy loss of £356 million; more than the entire cost of higher and further education in 1967-8. With the growing size and sophistication of international capital markets and especially the Euro-currency market, see also p. 183 below, the costs would now be many times larger. Indeed there is so much cash in the world's financial markets that it may be impossible to maintain a fixed parity or even a preferred level of exchange rate (see the discussion of the US's position in November 1979, p. 174 below, in which it is argued that even the US could not maintain the dollar's international value against the weight of market forces, even if they chose to).

Unfortunately this argument is not incompatible with the view that *floating rates have been inflationary*, for the world as a whole. There are a number of reasons why this may be so.

One group of arguments relies upon expectational factors, e.g. the argument of Machlup in Classen and Salin (1976). The author once summarised this view as follows:

> To the extent that a world inflationary psychology has now developed, inflation in one country intensifies inflationary expectations there and elsewhere, and thus renders it harder for any one country to fight the tide. It seems reasonably clear that floating rates reduce the barriers to the spread of inflation from one country to another and make it harder for one country to resist the climate of world inflation (as for example, West Germany, Belgium, Holland and Switzerland did in the mid-60s).
>
> (Gowland and Pakenham (1974))

A simpler argument relates floating rates and inflation by use of the ratchet argument that cost decreases are not as deflationary as cost increases are inflationary. Thus, if in the spring the pound falls against the mark, UK prices tend to rise but there is no counterbalancing fall in German prices. In the autumn the pound may recover, producing a rise in German prices but no fall in UK ones. Hence the fluctuations in exchange rates have left exchange rates at their original level but raised prices in both countries. For a full discussion of the relationship between exchange rates and domestic price, see section 10.1 below.

The nature of most of the arguments considered so far in this section has been such that firm conclusions were difficult to derive and rigorous analysis often had to give way to politico-economic speculation. The next two arguments, by contrast, are hard economic ones: uncertainty (9.4) and destabilising speculation (9.5). Some conclusions are then drawn (9.6).

9.4 Uncertainty and Exchange Rates

One of the longest-running arguments for fixed rates is that floating rates induce an extra uncertainty which reduces the volume of world trade. This reduction, moreover, involves an inefficient allocation of resources, since the reduction has been caused by an incentive to view two goods or markets differently simply because of their location.

This argument arises because international trade will apparently mean that at least one agent will have expenditure in one currency and receipts in another and so has an extra uncertainty about the value of his income. If Rowntree of York are considering whether or not to sell Yorkie bars in New York they will have to consider consumer demand, production costs and so on just as they would if they were selling Yorkie bars in Edinburgh. In addition, however, they must face the problem that Americans will pay for the bars in dollars, whereas Rowntree pay wages in pounds. With (fully) fixed rates this would not matter as Rowntree could easily calculate how many pounds their expected dollar revenue would buy. If exchange rates fluctuate they will not know the return in pounds from any given level of sales. If the dollar is higher than Rowntree expect, they will have an unexpected bonus, but if it is lower, their profits may be wiped out. If, as is conventional and reasonable, risk aversion is assumed, then Rowntree will dislike this extra factor that could affect profits and so will be inclined not to export when they otherwise would. Rowntree may not face the uncertainty themselves but someone will. For example, Rowntree may be paid in pounds by a US wholesaler. However, he will then have sterling expenditure and dollar receipts so he will be biased to purchase Hershey's products instead of Rowntree's.

This uncertainty about the value of export receipts, or the cost of imports, will act as a deterrent to trade that would improve the world's allocation of resources, or so the fixed rate proponents have argued since, at least, Ricardo. It is important to note, however, that it is an argument in favour of *fully* fixed rates. With adjustable parities there is a small probability of a large change in exchange rates. With dirty floating, there is a very high probability of a smaller change in exchange rates and a much smaller probability of a large change. It is not clear which would induce the greater uncertainty. Under Bretton Woods the American wholesaler's calculations might be: 'Unless there is a devaluation we will make £1 million more from Rowntree's than Hershey's products; if there is a devaluation we will make a loss (and would be £2 million better off with Hershey's). There is a 10 per cent chance of devaluation.' Under dirty floating, they might be 'We will be between £½ million and £1½ million better off with Rowntree's bars unless the exchange rate changes by more than 10 per cent. There is only a 1 per cent chance of that.'

In this example the wholesaler would be more likely to buy (British) imports under dirty floating since the risk of a catastrophic change in rates is much smaller even though uncertainty is greater in some sense (at least by conventional measures). It would be easy to construct counter examples, but in fact what matters in all cases of uncertainty is whether it can be insured against and at what cost. If there is a market in which insurance is available against the risk, then uncertainty itself will not reduce trade, only the insurance premium will. Sohmen (1969) argued that uncertainty about the value of receipts or expenditure would disappear if there were forward exchange markets. Moreover, because of the interest parity arbitrage described in 9.2, there would always be forward exchange markets.

Sohmen's first argument is incontrovertible. If Rowntree are able to sell forward dollars, or the American importer to buy forward sterling (the same transaction), there is no more risk to selling in New York than Edinburgh and no more risk in buying British than American chocolate bars. A forward sale or purchase can guarantee that receipts and expenditure are in the same currency. If Rowntree expect to sell one million Yorkie bars at 10 cents each, they can sell $100,000 forward and ensure a return of, say, £50,000 and compare this with the prospective return from selling the chocolate in Edinburgh and with the cost of making it, both of which are sterling outlays. Many uncertainties remain but none bias the choice towards one market rather than the other. If forward markets exist and are not used, the implication is that the uncertainty does not affect business decisions.

Sohmen's next proposition is more controversial, although theoretically impeccable. It is probably best to illustrate it with a specific example. If (American) dollar interest rates are 15 per cent p.a. and sterling (British) interest rates are 12 per cent p.a. and the spot rate is $2, the equilibrium forward rate is $2.054 (approximately). Sohmen's argument is designed to show that there will be a forward market, because it is risklessly profitable to offer forward cover. If a dealer were to offer to supply forward pounds at $2.1 and buy them at $2 for one year ahead, he would make a profit (of 10 cents) on any matching transactions — if Rowntree bought £1 million forward (i.e. sold $2.1 million) and Ford sold £1 million sterling forward (i.e. bought $2 million dollars) he would make $100,000 (which he could also take as £46,379 or as a mixture of pounds and dollars). If, instead, his book does not match — say he has contracted to supply £1 million forward — he can still guarantee a profit. He has contracted to pay out £1 million and will receive $2.1 million. If he borrows $1.8 million he will have to repay $2,070,000 ($1.8 million he borrowed plus $270,000 interest).

For $1.8 million he can buy £900,000 and invest it so that he receives £108,000 interest. Hence his borrowing, conversion and lending operation will leave him with an obligation to pay $2,070,000 and receipts of £1,108,000. This means that when he has paid out £1 million and received $2.1 million on the forward contract, he has a net profit of $30,000 and £8000 on an investment of zero. (He could obviously adjust the transaction to take all his profits in dollars, all in sterling, or various other combinations of them.)

More generally, so long as it is possible to borrow in one currency and lend in another, then, so long as there are spot exchange markets, it will always be possible to offer forward exchange at a riskless profit. Hence, Sohmen argues, forward exchange markets will always exist. (If they did not, hedging could be done on a home-made basis by a suitable borrowing, conversion and lending operation.)

Moreover, competition should drive the forward rate towards the equilibrium (i.e. someone else has an incentive to buy forward pounds at $2.01 and sell them at $2.09 and so on until the abnormal profit is eliminated). Sohmen's analysis makes two assumptions:

1. There is no default risk; the *arbitrageur* needs to be sure that no one defaults otherwise he is in terrible trouble. In practice, with large companies and large banks he can conduct all three transactions in complete safety.

2. The *arbitrageur* can borrow and lend in dollars at the same interest rate. If not, the difference between them adds a transaction cost, discussed below. In practice, banks are virtually the only dealers in forward exchange, because the margin between their borrowing and lending rates is so much less (perhaps negative!) than anyone else's.

The first problem with Sohmen's argument is that there is not a complete set of forward markets, especially for the far distant future — and after all if Rowntree were thinking of building a factory to supply New York they might want to sell dollars forward ten years ahead. As one commentator puts it: 'Do they work? Usually but not always . . . [sometimes] the market stops functioning just because it's a market' (Smith, 1982).

However, with the growth of Eurocurrency markets, many more forward markets exist than used to be the case. Of course, governments may not permit their residents to use the markets even if they exist, but legalisation of such transactions is the best way of removing the exchange rate uncertainty implied in international trade. For example, 'foreign currency surcharges' were at one time a common danger of booking a foreign holiday for UK residents, until the Bank of England permitted the package holiday industry to use the forward market, in 1978.

A more serious problem with the simple analysis above is that it ignores transactions costs. The arbitrage transaction will increase costs – if only by a few phone calls. Hence forward cover may always be available, but at a cost. This transaction cost will inhibit international trade in the same way as more obvious transport costs.

However, it makes it possible to assess alternatives, like 'dirty floating' and adjustable parities in terms of the effective cost of forward cover. *Ceteris paribus*, the uncertainty argument is an argument for the regime where forward cover is cheapest. In fact dirty floating involves a cost about three times that of adjustable parities. Of course, this is not a decisive consideration but the uncertainty argument can be reduced to an argument about the cost of removing it – and this is measurable.

9.5 Speculation

Arguments about speculation are either arguments for fully fixed exchange rates or, more relevantly, concern the case for some intervention by governments in foreign exchange markets. There would be no speculation if exchange rates were truly fixed for ever. However, this is obviously irrelevant to the real world since, even if a fully fixed system were introduced, it would be many years before all participants became convinced that rates would never change. More relevantly, it is alleged that if governments did not intervene, speculators would carry out transactions that would produce undesirable movements in exchange rates. In particular, speculation might be destabilising, that is, it might lead to larger fluctuations in the exchange rate than would otherwise occur. This would be an argument against free floating. Destabilising speculation would not in itself justify one system of intervention rather than another and does not provide an argument for 'fixed' against 'floating' rates in general. Indeed the reverse could be true, since adjustable parities encourage speculation by providing one-way options.

Friedman (1953) argued that destabilising speculation was impossible and that the effects of speculation would be desirable. His argument has been extended to defend speculation in all markets, invoking a tart comment from Galbraith that it was like a harlot arguing that she was a good cook (Galbraith (1953), p.137). Friedman argues that speculation will only persist if it is profitable. In any case unprofitable speculation is unlikely to be harmful; why worry if imports and exporters, or even *arbitrageurs*, gain at the expense of speculators? In fact losing speculation can persist, e.g. financed by profits from other income or by new inflows of funds, in the case of, for example, a pension fund. In fact it is quite likely that it would, since a few speculators would profit even if most lost and this would almost certainly ensure that speculation remained popular — as with any other form of gambling. (See Gowland (1982a), pp. 149-51 for a discussion of a similar problem.)

Nevertheless, Friedman's premises are acceptable. Speculation is not necessarily harmful and it would only be if there were profitable, destabilising speculation that serious problems would arise. Speculation will be profitable only if the average buying price is less than the average selling price. Such speculation will tend to iron out price fluctuations, not accentuate them.

This argument is simplest when there is a trend value of the exchange rate and the actual exchange rate varies around this trend. If speculators enter the market, they can profit by buying when price is below trend and selling when it is above but, in this case, they will increase demand relative to supply and so increase price when price is below trend; and reduce demand relative to supply, i.e. be net suppliers, when price is above trend and so reduce price. Hence, they will tend to bring the price closer to the trend.

They can profit in other ways, e.g. by buying when price is a long way below trend and selling when it is closer to trend, but all will move price closer towards the (equilibrium) trend value. Perfect speculation would ensure that the actual value was always equal to the long-run trend value. Effectively, some rational expectations models assume that this is the case.

Friedman's argument is incontrovertible so long as two assumptions are valid:

1. *The long run value of the currency is independent of short-term fluctuations in the exchange rate.* In the context above, this would mean that the trend was independent of any fluctuations round it. More generally it would mean that any speculator-induced deviation from equilibrium was not permanent. For example, if short-selling speculators drove the pound down from $1.80 to $1.20, they would necessarily lose when the rate rebounded. However if $1.20 became the

new equilibrium rate, they could cover their short sales and so profit. In this case the speculator-dominated market would have a totally different path of exchange rates from the path that would otherwise prevail and might be more or less variable. If exchange rates influence the rate of inflation, Friedman's assumption is not valid.

2. *The market is stable in the technical sense.* In Friedman's two-equation model, the stability condition is that the slope of the demand curve is less than that of the supply curve; it automatically is, of course, if the demand curve is downward-sloping (i.e. negatively sloped), and the supply curve upward-sloping. In the foreign exchange market there are both theoretical arguments and empirical evidence which suggest that the demand curve for currency might be upward-sloping in the short run. However, the more serious objection to Friedman's assumption is that his model is over-simple and that a more sophisticated model is necessary. In the multi-equation models of the foreign exchange market that have been devised, stability conditions are more complex and are by no means *a priori* valid.

Technical instability could justify intervention by itself. If a deviation from equilibrium will lead to an exchange rate that moves further and further away from the equilibrium path, the case for intervention seems very strong. The counter-argument is that rates do not either explode upwards or drop to zero — but this is not decisive because intervention is the norm.

Hence whilst Friedman's argument is valid on its own terms, it is, nevertheless, not clear that destabilising speculation is *a priori* impossible. Considerable efforts have been made to see whether destabilising speculation exists but the overall results have been inconclusive. This may be because destabilising speculation sometimes exists and/or is profitable and at other times does not.

In any case it is probably true that destabilising speculation is caused by official intervention, whether or not it would otherwise occur. The argument is simple. The classic act of a destabilising speculator is to buy when price has risen and sell when it has fallen. Official intervention often seeks to 'smooth' the market, to narrow the day-to-day movement of rates. This may justify destabilising speculation — the speculator can calculate: 'The pound has risen 2 cents and the Bank of England has probably intervened to stop it rising by more (a smoothing operation), so without the intervention it would have risen 4 cents, so I will buy as it is more likely than not to rise the other 2 cents tomorrow.'

If the destabilising speculation that occurs in the real world is (even partially) caused by intervention, it is impossible to determine whether it would occur without such intervention. Hence, one cannot say whether or not destabilising speculation justifies intervention. This conclusion may seem a little inconclusive and in a sense it is, so conclusions are usually formed by more fundamental views. It cannot be shown that intervention is either necessary or unnecessarily harmful. Hence, the question becomes one of how well markets are likely to work.

9.6 Some Conclusions

In the author's opinion, no government should, or even could, renounce intervention in the foreign exchange market because of the impact of exchange rate variations on the economy. Only the US is exempt from this and, even there, as the economy becomes more open it is less immune to the effects of exchange rate variations on employment and prices. As the exchange rate will not produce balance of payments equilibrium by itself, it is better used as a tool of domestic policy, at least partly. Even if it is accepted that quasi-constitutional devices are needed to curb public spending, a rigid exchange rate seems an indirect and ineffective method of achieving it; a direct limit on government spending or a balanced-budget constitutional rule seem both more likely to work in practice and likely to achieve the goal of the 'discipline' school. (Ignoring all other considerations, if public servants know that issuing public sector pay cheques is a criminal offence in some circumstances, it gives both those who issue and those who receive the cheques an enormous incentive to see that the circumstances do not arise, i.e. the budget remains balanced or that public spending is below its ceiling.)

Because of 'one-way options', dirty floating is inevitably the only interventionist regime that is practicable and it may well be optimal for the 1970s and 1980s even if more choice were available. Uncertainty can best be reduced by ensuring that forward markets operate as widely and cheaply as possible and that their services are well known to potential beneficiaries. It is, however, perhaps best to end this chapter by stressing how maladroit official intervention in foreign exchange markets has often been, e.g. that by the UK in 1975-6. If there is a case for freely floating rates it is (the familiar argument) that while markets may fail, official intervention is costly and often ineffectual.

Note

1. The UK convention is to define exchange rate as the number of units of foreign currency obtained for each unit of domestic currency, e.g. x dollars per pound. In the US the convention is to define the exchange rate as the number of units of domestic currency required to purchase one unit of foreign currency, e.g. pence per dollar. The two are the reciprocal of each other.

10 THE EXCHANGE RATE AND ECONOMIC POLICY

10.1 Introduction: The UK 1974-82

Balance of payments theory was considered in Chapters 6 to 8 and the exchange rate in Chapter 9. This chapter seeks to integrate the analysis of these four chapters so as to extend the analysis and, especially, to highlight the main considerations which influence economic policy in medium-sized open economies such as the UK. In apparently paradoxical contradiction to the conventional wisdom of the 1960s, modern theories suggest that the main determinant of the balance of payments is domestic macroeconomic policy, especially the level of government spending, and the level of domestic credit expansion on which it is the major influence. On the other hand, the exchange rate is important primarily as an influence upon the level of employment and the price level.

The simplest of such models is the one which seems to have had most influence upon the UK government. This is the proposition that the exchange rate is inversely related to the level of nominal income, i.e. price times output. A depreciation will increase nominal income. *Ceteris paribus*, this should increase output and so should reduce unemployment, even though the rate of increase of prices will rise. An appreciation will contrariwise reduce nominal income below the level it otherwise would be and so reduce inflation, even though unemployment will rise. Indeed, the conventional unemployment-inflation trade-off presents itself most clearly in the UK in the context of exchange rate policy.

The relationship between the exchange rate and nominal income can be established by either elementary monetarist or basic Keynesian analysis. The monetarist analysis is that the exchange rate directly influences the money supply through the overseas impact on the money supply – see Gowland (1982a), pp. 47-8, for a detailed explanation of the mechanism involved. A change in the money supply necessarily causes an equivalent change in nominal income in the orthodox monetarist model. The Keynesian mechanism is that the balance of payments is improved at each level of income, hence planned injections (X + I + G) are higher relative to planned withdrawals (S + M + T) at each level of income. Therefore the equilibrium level of nominal income is higher.

This analysis was shown on p. 88 above and, in a special case of the mechanism, in the examination of the New Cambridge school on p. 99 above. These propositions about the inverse relationship between nominal income and the exchange rate make it possible to explain both the gyrations of UK exchange rate policy over the last decade and a major difference between Mrs Thatcher's economic policies and those advocated by Peter Shore as part of Labour's 'Alternative Economic Strategy'.

The Labour government of 1974-9 sought a high exchange rate to reduce inflation whenever incomes policy was unsuccessful (1974-5 and 1977-8) and a lower rate to reduce unemployment whenever it seemed that incomes policy was curbing inflation (the early part of 1976). The Labour government's use of the exchange rate as an instrument of fine-tuning was controversial. In 1974-5 wages were soaring and unemployment was low, so the government sought to hold the exchange rate up as an anti-inflationary device. This was not too difficult because of the aftermath of the 1973 oil crisis which meant that OPEC funds poured into London. Nevertheless, it added to the pressure on corporate liquidity which so frightened Mr Healey as to produce the dramatic U-turn of the November 1974 Budget. In the early part of 1976, with a successful incomes policy and rising unemployment, the government sought a lower exchange rate to reduce unemployment. However, the attempt was disastrous in that it produced an uncontrollable and humiliating sterling crisis as the downward pressure on sterling accelerated. In 1977-8, a higher rate was at least tolerated both to reduce monetary growth and to assist a faltering incomes policy. Other more minor changes in exchange rate strategy were common. In fact, it sometimes seemed that the exchange rate was the only instrument of fine-tuning that this government permitted itself to use. The execution of the policy was marked by some very strange, indeed apparently illogical, dealing tactics (Gowland (1982a), p. 168). Moreover, the exchange rate seems at least as open as any other instrument of policy to the conventional criticisms of fine-tuning. Indeed it may be even harder to use the exchange rate in an excessively active fashion than other instruments because of the effects on the expectations of those who deal in foreign exchange. In general, UK experience in this period confirms that while the exchange rate is a potentially useful tool of economic management, considerable care is needed in implementation and it is no easier to use than conventional monetary and fiscal instruments.

A similar verdict of 'controversial, imaginative but incompetently executed' may well be history's verdict upon the exchange rate policy of the present Conservative government in the UK, which seems to have regarded the exchange rate as a transmission mechanism for its monetary policies (see Gowland (1982a), p. 186). The government's hope was that the effect of the exchange rate, both directly and via its effect on the money supply, would help to squeeze corporate liquidity and so reduce corporate spending, in particular to reduce the wage bill by reducing the wages per employee (below the level they otherwise would be). Some effect on output was anticipated, but it was believed that much of the effect of monetary policy would be on prices. Instead, corporate spending was also reduced by reducing employment and by reducing stock levels. In addition companies borrowed heavily from banks to offset the squeeze on their liquidity and so thwarted the objective of monetary restriction. Moreover, the reduction in stocks and in the numbers employed ensured that more of the remaining effects of monetary policy were on output than on price. This use of the exchange rate as both an instrument and transmission mechanism of monetary policy has been highly controversial – see Gould *et al*. (1981) for a savage partisan critique. Nevertheless, the policy was logically planned and reflected a keen awareness of the impact of exchange rates on the domestic economy. Moreover, there is some support for the policy in the Bank of England's model of the economy in which exchange rates are the main transmission mechanism of monetary policy (Bank (1979)). The execution of the policy was, however, much less imaginative than the design.

In 1981-2, as the level of unemployment rose, the goverment became less enthusiastic about a high exchange rate and a slow drift down of the exchange rate was tolerated and even welcomed in some quarters. The issue became very topical in early December 1982. The pound came under very heavy pressure (and lost abut 7 per cent of its value, in terms of foreign exchange, in a week). This was partly inspired by an article in the *Sunday Times* (5 December), alleging that the government's Chief Economic Adviser wanted a depreciation to reduce unemployment. By coincidence, in the same week, the Shadow Chancellor unveiled Labour's economic policy, of which a key element was a 30 per cent depreciation of sterling to reduce unemployment. Mrs Thatcher responded with a speech (Friday, 10 December) in which she re-avowed her opposition to a lower exchange rate because it would mean a higher level of prices.

10.2 The Small Economy Model

Besides the indirect effect of the exchange rate on prices and employment considered above, there may also be direct effects. The simplest of these direct effects can best be analysed in the context of a small economy (see p. 112 above). This stems from the undoubted fact that a change in the price of competing goods will change the behaviour of the suppliers. If the price of Fiats and Renaults rises, BL are likely to take the opportunity to raise the price of their cars. The only question is by how much; there is no conceivable microeconomic theory which would deny some increase, although the traditional analysis argues that the effect is trivial. In a small economy where domestic producers are price takers at the world price, the analysis is simple, as all domestic producers face a horizontal marginal revenue curve at the world price expressed in the domestic currency, i.e. the dollar price divided by the exchange rate. When the exchange rate changes there will be an equivalent (but opposite) change in the price level, such that a 1 per cent appreciation will lead approximately to a 1 per cent fall in domestic prices. The mechanism is simple and is illustrated in Figure 10.1(a). This shows the cost and revenue curves for a typical producer of a good, say, leets, of which the world price is \$1. Initially, the exchange rate is \$2 = £1 so producers of leets face a horizontal marginal revenue curve at 50p (which is also their average revenue and demand curve), i.e. at the world price expressed in sterling. If the exchange rate falls to \$1 = £1, the marginal revenue curve shifts upwards to £1 (\$1 divided by the new exchange rate), but is still horizontal. The equilibrium price is now p_2 (£1) instead of p_1 (50p) and output has risen from q_1 to q_2 so presumably the firm is employing more workers. Hence the representative firm will raise its output, employment and price. As the same diagram illustrates every firm in the economy, the result can be generalised to a rise in aggregate output, a higher rate of inflation and a lower level of unemployment. This analysis led, in the 1960s, to a discussion of profit elasticities because, in the case of a small economy, the analysis had to concentrate on the effect of a change in profits on output and so on the balance of payments, rather than examine the impact of changes in relative prices. This concept can easily be incorporated into the absorption approach; in which case depreciation could increase output, as well as expenditure.

This 'small economy' case, however, ignores the fact that a change in the exchange rate will affect costs. For an individual firm, costs can be divided into wages, purchases from abroad and purchases of domestic

Figure 10.1: A Small Economy

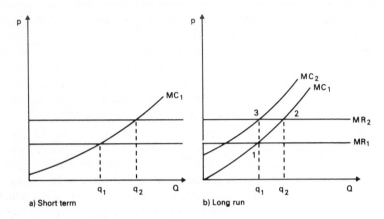

a) Short term

b) Long run

Depreciation increases output only in the short term

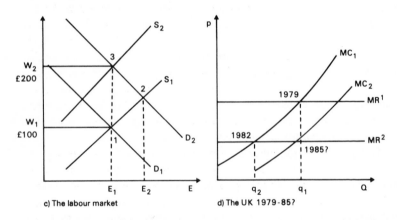

c) The labour market

d) The UK 1979-85?

inputs. However, by familiar national income analysis, the latter costs can in turn be decomposed until all costs are either wages or purchases of imports. The domestic currency price of imports will rise *pari passu* with the depreciation and so shift the marginal cost upwards. If all costs were outlays on imports, the marginal cost curve would shift from MC_1 to MC_2 in Figure 10.1(b) such that the output fell to the original level. This shift would occur because the upward parallel movement in the marginal cost curve would be exactly the same as in the price level. Thus, there will only be a long-term increase in output if wages rise by less than the price of imports, i.e. by less than the price level. This is a restatement of Johnson's proposition discussed above (p. 113) that devaluation has to reduce real wages if it is to improve the balance of payments. However, unless there is money illusion, on conventional assumptions, wages will rise by the same amount as prices. If the supply of labour is a function of real wages, it will shift upwards following the rise in prices, as from S_1 to S_2 in Figure 10.1(c). The demand for labour is a derived demand and will shift outwards from D_1 to D_2, following the shift of the marginal revenue curve in 10.1(a). The shifts are such that wages will double (for the hypothetical halving of the exchange rate) and employment will return to the original level, E_1.

Hence, as wages per worker rise by the same amount as imports, Figure 10.1(b) represents the long-term reaction of the firm producing leets to a depreciation from $2 = £1 to $1 = £1. The firm's equilibrium moves over time from 1 to 2 to 3 on both 10.1(b) and 10.1(c) such that it originally charges 50p, produces q_1 and employs E_1 workers at £100 per week each. In the short term, the depreciation raises output to q_2 and employment to E_2 as well as price to £1, so (generalising) the higher price level has induced more jobs. However, the final equilibrium has q_1 output and E_1 jobs, so there is a doubling of wages and prices but no change in real magnitude. This can be generalised to a trade-off between a short-term unemployment and a permanent rise in employment of the type hypothesised by Friedman (for different reasons, see Gowland (1982b), Chapter 4). The Labour Party's argument for a 30 per cent depreciation could be presented within this framework but Peter Shore would no doubt argue that an incomes policy would be able to prevent wages from rising by as much as import prices.

This model can also be used to present the London Business School analysis of the UK economy, 1979-85, Figure 10.1(d). The effect of an appreciation is the mirror image of that of a depreciation. Thus, in the short term, the rise in the exchange rate in 1979-80 led to a fall in output and in inflation, i.e. the economy's position in 1982. However, in the long term (1985?), output will recover to its trend level. The London Business School, as a matter of prescription, seem to feel that the short-term output cost is excessive relative to the long-term inflation gain; at least their media presentations have argued that the exchange rate rose by too much in 1979-80. In this respect international monetarists then felt that Mrs Thatcher was over-restrictive, whereas orthodox monetarists felt that monetary growth was excessive. The 16 per cent fall in the UK exchange rate in the last three months of 1982 was equally controversial.

10.3 Exchange Rates, Wages and Prices in a Large Economy

In a large open economy there will still be a direct relationship between the exchange rate and the price level. There is no doubt that a depreciation will have an effect on the overall price level. Imports are a component of final demand, so as a depreciation, barring very strange circumstances, must increase the price of imports in domestic currency, it must increase the domestic price level. If imports are 40 per cent of final demand, a 10 per cent depreciation increases prices (GDP deflator or RPI) by 4 per cent, using a base-weighted price index. The controversy is about the effect on the prices of domestically produced goods. The change in the price of competing goods will also lead to a change in price as in the small economy, but in a more complex fashion. The demand curve for the products of most domestic firms will be downward sloping. A depreciation (appreciation) will shift this outwards (inwards), but not necessarily by a parallel amount nor necessarily the same amount for each firm as in the small economy. Nevertheless, the direction of change is the same.

An equally simple result can be derived for oligopoly in which case either price leadership or conscious parallelism will lead to a similar matching of domestic to international price, so long as one (or more) importers are price leaders. Alternatively, the devaluation may act as a signal for a price change in more complex models. It is often argued that oligopolies require some signal before all firms are confident that rivals are likely to imitate a price increase. Depreciation is an almost perfect signal.

It is clear that a depreciation will raise the cost of imported inputs; raw materials, semi-manufactured and other intermediate goods. This rise in costs, shifting marginal cost curves to the right, will lead to a rise in price almost irrespective of assumptions about market situations and elasticity. The exception involves a bizarre (and probably illogical) combination of extreme cases, including perfectly inelastic demand and zero income elasticities. However, the rise in costs is unlikely to lead to a rise in prices by an amount equivalent to the depreciation. Costs rise by (the proportion of imported inputs to total costs) times (depreciation), i.e. only by a fraction of the depreciation. Prices themselves will rarely rise by as much as costs.

The cost effect could interact with the demand effect above to produce a price rise as large as, or even larger than, the depreciation. To obtain a substantial independent cost effect, however, it is necessary to make additional assumptions. The best way of showing a *pari passu* cost effect is to use a 'cost-push' model of inflation in which trade unions bargain for real wages and can ensure that any rise in prices is matched by an equivalent rise in wages and in which firms pass on all cost increases, i.e. some form of mark-up pricing. In this case there will be an effect on domestic prices from both the rise in costs and the rise in price of imported final goods. Either would be sufficient to ensure a rise in prices equivalent to the depreciation. For simplicity each effect will be analysed separately, although they interact. If imports are 20 per cent of final consumption, then a 10 per cent depreciation will raise the price level by 2 per cent. This will lead to a rise of 2 per cent in wages which (as for simplicity it is assumed that there are no imported inputs) will lead to a rise of 2 per cent in the price of domestically produced goods, i.e. 1.6 per cent on the price level (domestically produced goods are 80 per cent of final consumption). Wages rise by 1.6 per cent and so on until wages and prices are both 10 per cent higher. More generally, if imports are $\frac{1}{z}$ of final consumption, prices rise by $(\frac{1}{z}.d)$ where d is the depreciation, then wages by $(\frac{1}{z}.d)$, prices by $(1 - \frac{1}{z})$ $(\frac{1}{z}.d)$, wages by this amount and so on. The eventual change in prices is the sum to infinity of a geometric series, whose initial term is $(\frac{1}{z}.d)$ and whose common ratio is $(1 - \frac{1}{z})$. This sum is d. Alternatively, if all of $(C + I + G)$ is domestically produced, but imports are $\frac{1}{y}$ of costs and wages, therefore $(1 - \frac{1}{y})$ of costs, then prices rise by $\frac{d}{y}$, wages by $\frac{d}{y}$, prices by $\frac{d}{y}(1 - \frac{1}{y})$, etc. Here the sum to infinity is again d. In fact both effects work together, but prices and wages will both rise by the same amount.

Similar results which do not rely on a cost-push model can be generated by a relationship between expected inflation and past change in prices, i.e. the standard modern model of inflation introduced by Friedman (see Gowland (1982b), Chapter 4). In this case the depreciation, by increasing the price level, raises inflationary expectations and so, *ceteris paribus*, both wages and prices. Depending upon the nature of the expectations formation mechanism and any second-round effects, prices may rise by less than, as much as, or more than the depreciation. Indeed a devaluation could set off persistent inflation, as Laidler and Parkin (e.g. 1975) argued that the 1967 devaluation in the UK did.

Both the cost-push and expectations approaches may involve assumptions about trade union behaviour, although they can be derived from competitive models as well. Indeed, it can generally be argued that the response of trade unions to the rise in prices is crucial to the analysis of the effects of a devaluation. *If trade unions ensure that real wages remain constant a devaluation cannot increase competitiveness* and all prices must rise by the amount of the depreciation in large economies just as they do in small ones. Similar results follow if labour markets are competitive so long as the supply of labour is a function of real wages. It has therefore frequently been argued that *devaluation or depreciation can influence competitiveness only if there is money illusion* (see p. 142 above), otherwise the depreciation will change behaviour in such a way that it generates equal rises in all wages and prices.

Attempts have been made to deny this, but none are very convincing. One argument is that trade unions (or atomistic workers) might accept a change in the exchange rate as a signal that real wages must fall. It has also been agued that an incomes policy would prevent the rises in wages predicted by economic analysis. The snag here, even ignoring historical evidence to the contrary, is that, if trade unions will accept a reduction in real wages, the gain in competitiveness will be achieved anyway and it is impossible to see why it should be easier to negotiate an incomes policy with a depreciation than without; common sense suggests the reverse. After all, a rise in the price level is not the ideal accompaniment to an incomes policy.

In general then, it seems that a depreciation will have a substantial direct effect on prices which will probably bring about at least as large a price rise as the depreciation. There are two important qualifications to be made: one is that the effects of an appreciation may not be as anti-inflationary as the effects of a depreciation are inflationary, and that, as a depreciation may bring about a short-term gain in competitiveness, successive, and increasing, depreciation might secure a permanent gain – at the price of accelerating inflation. France pursued such a policy with some success between 1949 and 1958 (excepting the period of Pinay's premiership). Timing is considered further in section 10.5 below.

Nevertheless, analysis of a large economy reinforces the small economy conclusions about the trade-off problem inherent in exchange rate policy. A decision about the optimal exchange rate reflects the valuation of the short-term level of employment against the long-term level of inflation.

10.4 The Scandinavian Model of Inflation

The analysis above did not distinguish between traded and non-traded goods, that is goods which do and do not face international competition. Obviously the distinction is over-simplified but it can be argued that the response of a chemical firm and a restaurant to devaluation is different, although cost-push and wage factors are common to both. A lot of modern research has gone into the analysis of such effects. One offshoot of this is the so-called Scandinavian model of inflation. This is a two-sector model of the economy in which there is a traded goods sector and a sheltered sector. The traded goods or open sector is subject to international competition and is a price taker at the prevailing world price. The sheltered sector, comprising non-traded goods and the public sector, sets wages according to the prevailing level in the traded goods sector and prices. Its prices are merely a mark-up over costs.

In this model, a depreciation leads to a *pari passu* increase in prices in the traded goods sector. As factors are paid their marginal revenue product in the open sector, wages will rise by the same amount. As prices and wages in alternative employment have both risen, there is an increase in wages in the sheltered sector. This leads to an increase in sheltered sector prices and so to further wage increases. A wage-price spiral ensues until wages and prices have risen by as much as in the open sector. The practical relevance of this model is questionable. The author is a sceptic, but it is presented both because it is a further example of the impact of exchange rates on the economy and because it shows how easily one can combine parts of different models to produce an allegedly more realistic whole: the open sector is an international monetarist model and the sheltered sector is a pure cost-push model.

10.5 The 'J' Curve Model

There are two reasons for analysis of the 'J' curve model. One is that it extends the analysis of the previous sections in considering the inter-relationship between domestic prices and the exchange rate. Further, it is an explicitly dynamic model of the balance of payments. The absorption and traditional theories were only comparative static models of equilibrium and, while the monetary theory was a model of disequilibrium, it was certainly not dynamic. The model is set out in Figure 10.2 which traces the movement of the balance of payments over time. The path approximates to the letter 'J' — hence the name of the model. The model is basically a dynamic version of the traditional elasticities theory; it does not incorporate income or monetary effects, but it does incorporate the direct effects of 10.1 above. The times cited are from former versions of the Treasury model (see Gowland (1979), pp. 51 and 73).

Figure 10.2: 'The 'J' Curve

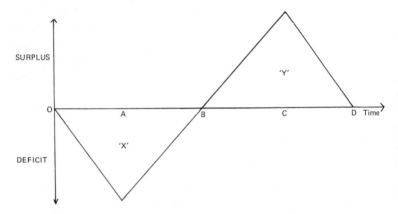

At time O the government devalues or provokes a depreciation of its currency. Initially the balance of payments worsens, the deterioration continues until 'A', about three months in the case of the UK. The reason for this deterioration is that in the short term volumes are fixed, by contractual or other relationships. Morever it is assumed that most, if not all exports are invoiced in the currency of origin. (This seems to be a valid assumption, see Williamson, Wood and Carse (1980).) That is, UK exports are priced in sterling, German exports (UK imports) in Marks, etc. Together, the two factors mean that the sterling value of exports is fixed (so the foreign currency value falls). The foreign currency value of imports is also fixed, so the sterling value rises. Thus, whether the balance of payments is measured in sterling or in a foreign currency, it deteriorates because, as the short-term elasticities are taken to be zero for contractual or other reasons,the Marshall-Lerner condition is not fulfilled.

After 'A', the balance of payments improves as volumes adjust to the new relative prices, at least if Marshall-Lerner is satisfied. After 'B' the effect is positive. ('B' is at about nine months according to those who estimated 'J' curves for the UK.) After a while, however, the rises in costs, expectations and the rest start to erode the gain in competitiveness. Hence the improvement reaches a peak at 'C' (15 months). Thereafter, the balance of payments deteriorates until at 'D' (27 months) it is back to its original level. However, while the long-run effect on the balance of payments is zero, there is an effect on the reserves (or UK holdings of overseas assets). From O – C, a cumulative deficit of X was experienced, compared, that is, to the position if there had been no depreciation. From C – D a surplus of Y was experienced, again compared to the no depreciation position. Thus there has been a net improvement in the cumulative current balance of (Y – X); (Y – X) could be negative but this is unlikely if the estimates of 'A', 'B', 'C' and 'D' cited above are accurate.

This 'J' curve model is special in that it assumes an exact relationship between depreciation and increases in domestic prices; e.g. the Laidler-Parkin argument is denied. It also assumes that trade flows respond faster to price changes than trade unions. It is possible to produce variants of 'J' curves in which effects are permanent and usually negative, or in which the balance of payments is always worse than if there had been no depreciation (see Gowland (1979), p. 50). Either would increase the instability of the foreign exchange market and justify intervention (see p. 135 above). An optimist could use 'J' curve analysis to justify a devaluation every 15 months; the balance of payments would always be better after the first nine months; but he or she would need nerves of steel since a slight miscalculation or variation in the parameters of the model and the balance of payments would always be worse.

10.6 Devaluation and the Terms of Trade

The terms of trade are the opportunity cost of imports in terms of exports, that is their relative price measured in the same currency. There has been much debate about the effect of depreciation of the currency on the terms of trade. The argument depreciation reduced real income by worsening the terms of trade was advanced as an argument against devaluation in the 1960s in the UK (see Beckerman (1972), p. 16). It has been advanced as an argument in favour of tariffs rather than devaluation as a device to improve the balance of payments that the former improves and the latter worsens the terms of trade, and that this difference outweighs any welfare effects of a tariff.

The effect of a devaluation or any other depreciation on the terms of trade depends upon the effect of the depreciation upon the domestic price level and the price of exports. If the price of all domestically produced goods including exports rises by as much as the (domestic currency) price of imports, there cannot be a change in the terms of trade. In the case of a small economy, by definition unable to change its terms of trade, a depreciation necessarily raises export prices (and domestic import substitutes) by the amount equivalent to the depreciation. In the case of a large economy, a depreciation, according to traditional analysis, necessarily worsened the terms of trade, by lowering the foreign currency price of exports leaving the foreign currency price of imports unchanged (or increasing the domestic currency price of imports leaving export prices constant). More modern analysis as predicted above suggests that while this is possible it may be only a short-term phenomenon.

10.7 Optimal Currency Areas

The relationship between exchange rates and unemployment led to the concept of an optimal currency area largely pioneered by McKinnon, e.g. in Cooper (1969) pp. 223-36. The subsequent literature may often seem arcane but it has been usefully applied both to the EEC and in analysing regional policy. The concept is based on the valid notion that, in effect, fully fixed exchange rates create a common currency. If two currencies are fixed for ever and are believed to be fixed for ever, there is no difference between holding one and the other. It is simply a matter of convenience, like a decision whether to have five one-pound notes or one five-pound note. Hence, an argument for a world-wide fully fixed exchange rate regime is an argument for a common world currency. The optimal currency area literature seeks to find criteria to decide what is the right area within which there should be a common currency, or fixed exchange rate. This might be wider than or smaller than existing nation states. McKinnon based his criteria largely on factor mobility. Exchange rates should be fixed within the area within which factors are immobile. Since then wider criteria have been developed.

It is argued that regional problems have been aggravated or even caused by over-large currency areas. The north-east of England, or Puerto Rico, might have less unemployment if they had their own currencies. Separate currencies for the 'snow' and 'sun' belts might have reduced the adjustment costs experienced in the US since 1970 by the faster growth of the latter relative to the former. If a region has a balance of payments deficit with the rest of the country, this will cause unemployment. If the area were able to reduce its real wages, or if labour were mobile, then the unemployment would be eliminated by an inflow of capital and/or an outflow of labour. In practice neither happens for obvious reasons and the cumulative process of deflation and balance of payments deficits continues – so it is argued – for centuries. If the north-east region could devalue the Tyneside pound against the London and Yorkshire pounds, this might, according to one's preferred theory, achieve all or any of the following: reduce real wages; eliminate the deficit; boost real income in Tyneside. In any case it would eliminate the problem. Within a nation state separate currencies are impossible, but it has been argued that labour subsidies might be a substitute for devaluation. 'Surplus' regions suffer unnecessary inflation in consequence of an inappropriate link, since the surplus earned by the south-east will lead to inflation by the inverse of the reason why Tyneside's deficit causes unemployment.

The argument is relevant to those currency unions which transcend national boundaries. In January 1979 the Republic of Ireland broke the link with sterling which had existed since 1921 because it believed Irish economic problems would be eased (a £600 million douceur from Germany and the EEC commission may also have influenced this action). According to the *Economist* (10 August 1982) powerful forces within Luxemburg wish to break the link with the Belgian franc; in this case Luxemburg is a net exporter but suffers (Belgian) inflation in consequence. Critics of the EEC's desire to create a common currency believe it would cause mass unemployment outside the 'golden triangle' (Paris basin, Ruhr, Rhine Valley and possibly that part of northern Italy near the Transalpine tunnels).

Note

1. For larger depreciations, the equivalent, or *pari passu*, increase in prices is not the same as the depreciation. If the exchange rate falls from $2 = £1 to $1 = £1, this is a 50 per cent depreciation, but the sterling price of American goods will double, because $1 is worth £1 instead of 50 cents. Thus the appreciation of the dollar is 100 per cent for a 50 per cent depreciation of sterling. An equivalent rise in prices is by the amount of the appreciation of the foreign currency (dollar) not the depreciation of the home currency (sterling), i.e. by the amount by which the price of foreign goods rises in sterling.

11 INTERNATIONAL FINANCE

11.1 Introduction

International finance is concerned with the mechanics of international transactions. Thus, in Chapters 9 and 10 there was a discussion of the goals of foreign exchange policy but in this chapter (11.2) the means of intervention are considered. Much of international finance is concerned with loans, so the availability of credit to nations, and the size of their reserves, is the crucial issue in international finance (11.3). This leads to a discussion of the demand for reserves (11.4). In Chapters 12 and 13 specific institutional arrangements are discussed, broadly the public sector ones in Chapter 12 and the private sector in Chapter 13.

11.2 Methods of Speculation and Intervention

Speculation and intervention have been discussed above but there was no consideration of how speculation or intervention are executed. Speculation can be defined as any transaction designed to yield a profit in the event that the exchange rate changes in the direction predicted by the speculator. *En passant*, such a transaction is no more irrational or wicked than any other profit-maximising act. Intervention is any operation carried out by a government designed to lead to a level of exchange rate different to that which would otherwise occur. Strictly and logically, a tariff, exchange control or even alterations in long-term interest rates, taxation and monetary policy might be called means of intervention, since they should all influence the exchange rate through the balance of payments. However, they are not conventionally thought of in this way so in this discussion intervention will be restricted to devices which will affect the exchange rate without any change in the basic or overall balance of payments, current account plus long-term capital. Most of the means of speculation parallel those of intervention. This arises in part because intervention is designed to reduce (or offset the effect of) speculation and also because in a sense intervention and speculation are the same thing, but with different motives and executed by different agents.

Both speculation and intervention can occur in the *spot market*. The speculator sells his holdings of the currency whose value he expects to fall and buys that which he expects to rise. He will normally choose to invest the proceeds in a bank deposit or other security denominated in the relevant currency. This procedure has obvious disadvantages. It is impossible to speculate 'against' a currency not already held. However certain you are that the lira will fall against the dollar, you cannot profit from this belief by spot market speculation unless you hold lira to sell. Moreover, the amount of speculation is limited to the speculator's wealth and, in practice. to his holdings of liquid assets. A company is unlikely, may be unable to, sell some of its UK assets merely to speculate against the pound. It is ludicrous, for example, to imagine Ford selling Dagenham because they wish to engage in foreign speculation. In general then, spot market speculation is rigid, limited in extent and, therefore, not very common.

As a means of intervention, there are similar limits to the use of the spot market. A government, or its central bank, can use its foreign exchange reserves to buy its currency or sell some of its own currency in exchange for foreign currency and thereby influence the price, i.e. the exchange rate. In practice such transactions usually involve either the purchase or sale of dollars. In the 1960s, by convention all intervention was in dollars; a convention very occasionally breached. Since 1970, the scale of intervention involving third currencies has grown, but it is still fairly small. The authority considering how to intervene faces restrictions similar to the speculator. It may not have very large foreign exchange reserves and it may not wish to use them. A large part of its reserves could be in currencies against which its exchange rate is at the desired level, so a sale would be undesirable. Alternatively, it might be viewed as an unfriendly act by the central bank of the currency concerned. If the UK is engaged in intervention to support the pound, a large sale of sterling by the Belgians to support their franc would not be very welcome. Central banks, on the whole successfully, seek to maintain good relations amongst themselves and so would not normally act in this way. A central bank/government could borrow the strong currency in order to sell it, but there are problems in doing this so alternatives are sought whenever possible. Obviously a central bank does not face any restriction on the amount of its own currency it sells; it can always create more. Nevertheless, this will lead to expansion of the money supply, which could easily wreck its monetary policy as the German, Swiss and UK authorities have all discovered. So, there are practical limits; in theory the money-creating effects of intervention can be sterilised by an equivalent offsetting open market operation. In practice sterilisation is rarely a viable operation.

Hence the authorities and the speculators would prefer an alternative forum for their operations. The most obvious is the *forward market*. The speculator can sell forward and profit, or lose, by any subsequent change in exchange rates. If, on 1 January, a speculator sells £1 million sterling forward for, say, delivery in three months at, e.g. $1.75, he is committed to delivering £1 million on 31 March. In exchange he will receive $1.75 million. If the spot exchange rate is $1.60, he can buy £1 million for $1.6 million and so make a profit of $150,000. (On the other hand, if the rate is $1.80 he makes a loss of $50,000.) The main problems of forward sales are the rigidity imposed by the fixed date of the contract and the fact that forward discounts are often very large on weak currencies, i.e. those expected to depreciate. The latter problem can be such as to eliminate any possibility of speculative profit − a 6 per cent forward discount is common, 10 per cent not unknown. The other disadvantage is that the contract can be exercised only on the named day. The spot exchange rate in the above example might be $1.70 on 28 March but $1.75 on 31 March so the speculator cannot profit, although right in his belief that sterling would fall. He might, if the spot and one-week forward rates (for simplicity) were both $1.70 on 24 March, either:

1. borrow $1.7 million spot and buy £1 million. He has then secured a profit of £50,000, less interest paid on his dollar loan plus interest he may receive on £1 million for a week;

2. buy £1 million forward for a week and so match his obligation to deliver £1 million on 31 March with a receipt of £1 million. His dollar obligation of $1.7 million is less than his dollar receipt of $1.75 million, so his profit is secure.

Both these are clumsy, however, and may not always be possible; there is no eleven-day forward market, for example. In this respect a forward market is less flexible than a *futures* or *options* market in which the right to buy or sell at a prescribed price on a specific day is traded. The right to buy £1 for $1.70 is worth 10 cents if the spot rate is $1.80, so, if on 1 January one expects a rate of $1.80 on 31 March, it would be worth paying 5 cents for the right to buy at $1.70. If in February the spot rate is $2, it should be possible to sell the option or 'future' for 15 or 20 cents. However, financial futures only came into existence in the mid-1970s, pioneered in Chicago, and the market was on an insigificant scale until 1980 and is still of limited scope. A private individual might be able to satisfy his requirements in this way but a large multi-national company could not and in any case transactions costs in this market are fairly substantial.

Central banks do not deal in futures but forward market intervention has been very common, following, but not necessarily because of, Keynes's prescription (1923). The argument for forward market intervention depends upon the existence of interest *arbitrageurs* (see p. 122 above). The basic *modus operandi* is to induce *arbitrageurs* to buy or sell your currency, since this secures the benefits of spot intervention without costs. A higher forward premium (or lower discount) will lead to increased demand for the currency and a lower forward premium (or bigger discount) to a reduced demand. *Ceteris paribus*, this change in demand should ensure a changed spot rate. These arguments will be illustrated by an example. Originally the interest parity condition is satisfied, with the dollar interest rate (RN) at 10 per cent, the sterling interest rate (RL) at 12 per cent, the spot rate at £1 = $2 and the one year forward rate £1 = $1.964. Both direct and indirect (see p. 121 above) investments in dollars yield 10 per cent and in sterling 12 per cent. The UK authorities now offer forward contracts in unlimited quantities at $1.98 = £1, i.e. they offer to agree to buy sterling offered in twelve months' time at $1.98. If an *arbitrageur* borrows $2 million he will have to repay $2.2 million in one year's time. He can convert the $2 million into £1 million and invest it so as to receive £1.12 million. If he sells £1.12 million forward he will receive $2,217,600. Hence he would make a net profit of $17,600. To obtain this he has taken advantage of the authorities' forward sterling purchases but, crucially, *he has bought £1 million of spot sterling.* This should raise the exchange rate until a new equilibrium is reached at about $2.017 = £1, when the interest parity condition is again satisfied. Hence, the authorities can influence the exchange rate without engaging in any spot transactions themselves.

Keynes ingeniously pointed out that this operation was costless if carried out on a sufficiently large scale. If the authorities peg the rate and then offer unlimited forward cover so as to maintain the rate for ever, they will never lose; indeed they will often make a large profit. In the above example, if by intervention in the forward market the rate is held at or above $2, then the authorities forward transactions yield a profit of over 2 cents per pound of transaction since they will buy in twelve months' time for $1.98 a pound worth at least $2. Unfortunately this Keynesian argument depends upon a virtually unlimited and successful operation. If the authorities chicken out or change their mind about the optimal rate, the cost can be staggering, for example if the rate cannot be held or if $1.80 becomes the optimal rate. In the real world, for example, nearly all the Bank of England's £356 million losses in 1967 were the result of forward market operations. The experience led a prominent central banker to say that Keynes's theory was like doubling up on black at roulette; it was theoretically impeccable but his nerves were not up to it. A further and crucial disadvantage of forward market operations is that they reduce the cost of forward market speculation, by reducing the forward discount on weak currencies and increasing the premium on strong ones.

Hence the forward market is not an ideal medium for either speculator or central bank. Therefore most speculation is now carried out via the overnight money markets. If a speculator borrows overnight in sterling, converts the proceeds into dollars and invests them in the overnight inter-bank dollar market, this offers an opportunity of profit if sterling depreciates, but involves the loss of the difference between the sterling interest rate and the dollar interest rate. Nevertheless, this loss is usually much lower than a comparable forward discount. This method is much more flexible than a forward contract, as one may renew the forward borrowing and lending daily. Thus the speculator has the chance to 'close out' his position on any day simply by not lending or borrowing for a further period.

Intervention by the authorities in the overnight inter-bank market is the most common technique, at least in the UK. By various devices, the authorities can engineer a squeeze in this market and force the interest rate up, often to over 100 per cent (see Gowland (1982a), p. 108). This directly raises the cost of speculation, since the speculator pays a higher rate on his borrowing. This is in marked contrast to forward market intervention which lowers the speculation costs. More importantly, the authorities will induce *arbitrageurs* to buy spot sterling (or sell it if the inter-bank rate is lowered). This time it is the domestic interest rate term in the parity equation which is raised and again the spot rate responds to arbitrage purchases, which should restore eqilibrium.

The last method of speculation, called '*leads and lags*', consists of deferring payments due to be made in a currency which is expected to depreciate (and accelerating them in one expected to appreciate). In this case a profit is made because, if the weak currency falls, the cost of paying one's bill is reduced. If one is due to pay £100 in June, when the exchange rate is $2, and actually pays in September, when it is $1, an American saves $100. Similarly a Briton due to pay $100 in September saves £50 by paying in June. Many holiday-makers practise this before going on holiday. If anyone purchases marks a few weeks in advance of a German holiday, or hangs on to marks for a few weeks after their return, they are hoping to profit from an exchange rate change. Similarly, if a purchase of lira for an Italian holiday is delayed until the last minute (or sterling travellers' cheques taken to Italy), this is a perfect example of lagging.

11.3 The Optimal Level of International Liquidity

The concept of international liquidity is not a very precise one but it has two main aspects:

1. the quantity of reserves held by all the world's central banks and/or governments;
2. the credit facilities open to them whereby they can borrow additional foreign currency.

Opinion has been sharply divided about whether the quantity of world liquidity has been inadequate. The largely Anglo-American school who believe that liquidity has been inadequate have proposed a variety of schemes to make available much easier and more extensive borrowing or to create extra reserves. The mechanism is sometimes complex but, in principle, international money can be created just as easily as a central bank can create domestic money. The other school believes that too much liquidity is already in existence and that the excess has produced very adverse effects.

The inadequate school have usually argued that liquidity is inadequate by using one of the following arguments:

1. *Liquidity is insufficient to finance international trade. In extremis*, someone wishes to buy something from, or sell something to, a non-resident but cannot because it is impossible to finance the transaction. Evidence of actual transactions that are not carried out because of a shortage of foreign exchange are rare but, in any case, usually it is assumed that (1) follows from either (2) or (3).
2. *Nations cannot finance (current account) balance of payments deficits*. The argument is that some nations, e.g. Britain in the 1960s or countries in the Third World, would like to have balance of payments deficits on current account but cannot borrow enough to have

them. Hence, they have to eliminate them in an unpalatable fashion. A variation of this is that they cannot finance a sufficiently long adjustment period. It might be optimal to eliminate a balance of payments deficit over five years, but if insufficient credit is available it may have to be eliminated in three years in a sub-optimal fashion.

3. *World liquidity has grown less fast than international trade.* This argument is that world liquidity is needed to finance world trade and that it has grown less quickly than world trade.

The counter argument starts by arguing that conventional measures of international liquidity are misleading because they take no account of the growth of the Eurocurrency market (see Chapter 13 below). Moreover, they then launch an all-out onslaught on the arguments of their opponents. The centrepiece of their argument is that *the insufficiency school has revived all the fallacies of the 'real bills' doctrine and so ignored all Keynesian and monetarist insights into economic behaviour.* The 'real bills' doctrine was the domestic equivalent of arguments (1), (2) and (3) above and was refuted by Ricardo in the early nineteenth century. No one tried to defend it in the UK after about 1850 nor in the US after the establishment of the Federal Reserve. The 'real bills' doctrine was that credit was insufficient if real transactions could not be financed, i.e. if there were insufficient credit for the 'needs of trade', to use an alternative term sometimes favoured by this group. The similarity to argument (1) above is obvious. Variants on (2) and (3) were also used by 'real bills' advocates; e.g. individuals and firms could not finance their deficits (e.g. investment plans that exceeded income) and that the money supply and/or volume of credit should grow as fast as nominal income. *The argument of the excess school is based on an application of very elementary macroeconomics to the world as a whole*, so it is best analysed by looking at the domestic case and then considering its wider application.

It is easy to refute the 'real bills' doctrine, that credit should always be available to finance a real transaction. A simple example concerns two bidders for a unique antique vase at an auction; a slightly unusual auction in that negotiations with bankers take place between bids. A bids £100 but B, who has only £50, can then legitimately approach his bank and say, "If you lend me £60 I will be able to buy the vase for £110.' This is a real transaction, so the loan is desirable according to the 'real bills' doctrine. A, with £100 cash, can then put exactly the same argument for a £20 loan to enable him to buy the vase for £120.

Then B could request a larger loan and so on *ad infinitum*. The only effect of easy credit is to drive the price of the vase ever higher. At all times one party is unable to finance a real transaction. More realistic examples are easy to construct, whereby loans to purchase goods drive the price of the good up. A real-world case is the UK housing market in 1972-3; see Gowland (1982a), pp. 128-34.

The monetarist therefore argues that the existence of a real trans-action is irrelevant to whether a loan is desirable. What matters is its effects upon the level of price and output. This is best measured by the quantity of money. Argument (3) is relevant here but clearly the money supply can grow less quickly than nominal income and still be infla-tionary, e.g. Germany in 1922-3.

The argument can be restated in a Keynesian style by looking at proposition (2) about the finance of deficits. A desire to run a deficit on current account means that the nation wishes to demand more goods than it supplies. If desired deficits exceed desired surpluses, there will be excess demand for goods which would mean a rise in price (or out-put). It is impossible for excess demand to be satisfied without a change in price and loans which create excess demand may be inflationary. The Keynesian version is even simpler. A planned surplus is a planned (net) withdrawal; a planned deficit is a planned (net) injection. Actual injec-tions will equal actual withdrawals. If plans are inconsistent, income will adjust to make them consistent. Hence, if planned deficits exceed planned surpluses, someone will have to change their plans. The plans may be changed by a lack of credit (as the deficiency school argue) or by a higher level of income. Whether it is desirable to extend credit depends upon whether the change in income is desirable.

Hence the 'excess' school argue rightly that the quantity of inter-national liquidity should be judged on macroeconomic criteria. A higher level of liquidity would increase world inflation but could also increase world output and employment. Opinions differ about whether the world balance of inflation and unemployment has been right or wrong and, in particular, about the extent to which inflation in the 1960s has caused unemployment since. The arguments are extensions of domestic macroeconomics and are left to the reader to resolve for himself or herself.

Some debates on world liquidity have been *ad hominem*. Germans, who would lose by inflation, have argued that the economists from the deficit nations (US and UK) have argued for policies which would bene-fit their own nations and vice versa. Polemics apart, this illustrates the genuine conflict of interest; the level of liquidity will be too high for a nation with a planned surplus when it is far too low for a nation with a planned deficit. A higher level of prices will put the costs on the former, a lower level of output on the latter.

Other arguments about the quantity of liquidity concern its distribution, both between different countries and different types of liquidity. The argument about distribution is that the overall quantity may be right but that some nations have too large a proportion of the world's liquidity and some too little. This is particularly relevant to Third World countries, who certainly have very little liquidity. However, the problem is one of insufficient wealth, income and resources rather than liquidity *per se*. Easy credit is not necessarily of much value to a poor nation; it may actually intensify its problems. These countries are not so much short of foreign currency as of the goods it could buy; an important distinction.

The argument about types of liquidity is more complex in that the same facts lead to opposite conclusions. There is an argument that, at least on occasions, an excessive proportion of world liquidity was in the form of dollars and that most nations held more dollars than they wanted. One group argued that the effective quantity of international liquidity was very much reduced. Comparison could be made with an internal bank failure. If a bank fails, its notes and deposits are worthless and an expansionary monetary policy is needed to deal with the problem.

The hard money school argued the reverse, citing Gresham's law, that international liquidity needed to be restricted. Nations would attempt to get rid of 'bad money' and would hang on to 'good', as Gresham argued, so only bad money would circulate. The attempt to dispose of bad money (dollars) would be inflationary. Restoring value to 'bad money' by a tighter US monetary policy was essential to the health of the system (see e.g. Smith (1982)).

11.4 The Demand for Reserves

The argument in 11.3 was that (domestic closed economy) macroeconomics should be applied to the world as a whole. In particular, elementary monetarist and Keynesian analysis was applied to the optimum quantity of liquidity. The logical extension seems to be to estimate a demand-for-reserves function so as to generate a world LM curve. Machlup has argued (1969) that the effort is pointless since the 'cloakroom theory' suffices. This is that nations will always want more reserves. The demand is for the previous level plus a small increase (the name is from an analogy with a woman who irrespective of the number of dresses in her wardrobe (cloakroom) would like one more). Less cynical economists have tried to estimate demand functions based on the conventional demand for money; Clark (1970), for example, attempted to apply a Tobin-Baumol model to the problem.

Utilising demand-for-money theory, one can group variables that might influence the demand for reserves according to the level of income/transactions; the return forgone by holding reserves and the rate of return on reserves, the opportunity cost and benefit of holding reserves.

1. *Income/Volume of transaction*
   (a)   GDP
   (b)   level of imports
   These are both straightforward.
2. *Rate of return on competitive assets*
   (a)   rate of return on real assets
   If a nation did not hold reserves it could use them to buy capital goods.
   (b)   rate of return on consumption
   As in (a), but the imports could be consumed. In this case the opportunity cost is the loss suffered by consuming later rather than now, the social rate of time preference (see Henderson (1969)).
   (c)   the rate of return on portfolio investment in the US
   (d)   long-term interest rates
   Any of (a) to (d) could be relevant depending upon what is perceived to be the alternative(s) to holding reserves.
3. *Rate of return on reserves*
   Reserves yield two benefits. The simplest is that they can earn interest if invested in a suitable medium, in practice this is
   (a)   US Treasury bill rate
   (b)   Eurodollar deposit rate
   (a) and (b) are comparable to the interest which is paid on bank deposits; the 'own rate'.
   The other benefit is that reserves can enable a nation to avoid having to deflate to remove a (current account) deficit. This benefit depends upon the cost of eliminating a deficit and its frequency.
4. *The marginal propensity to import*
   The cost of eliminating a deficit depends upon the marginal prospensity to import (MPM) since, in absorption theory, a deficit is eliminated by a change in expenditure equal to the reciprocal of the MPM times

the deficit (if the MPM = 0.2, a £500 million fall in expenditure is needed to reduce imports by £100 million).

5. *The variance of imports and/or exports*

If the long-run levels of exports and imports are equal, then short-run fluctuations in them will cause deficits. These are measured by such measures of dispersion as the variance.

Much work has been done to see which if any combination of these twelve variables best explains the observed pattern of reserve holding. The results are somewhat mixed but on the whole well-fitting functions have been discovered. It seems that the balance of payments variables (4 and 5) are relevant to the developed countries but not to the Third World. This suggests that Third World countries eliminate deficits by quantity controls (quotas, etc.) and do not use reserves to finance deficits. On the other hand, the transaction variables are relevant to Third World countries but not to the developed world. This suggests that the Third World Countries, or their citizens, do not have access to the sophisticated banking system which eliminates the need for transaction balances. Nevertheless, all such conclusions have proved to be of a tentative and preliminary nature.

12 THE INTERNATIONAL MONETARY SYSTEM

12.1 History

There are three major aspects to any international monetary system:

1. the exchange rate regime;
2. arrangements for co-operation between nations, in practice usually between their central bankers;
3. arrangements for loans to be extended to nations, either by other nations on a bilateral basis or multilaterally through an international agency.

Any analysis must concentrate on these, whether historical or descriptive or prescriptive. Analysts may also wish to differentiate between the way the system works and the formal mechanism, rather as constitutional scholars since Bagehot have distinguished the 'efficient' from the 'dignified', the reality from the formal system.

The modern history of the international monetary system starts with the Bretton Woods conference of 1944, which was a major part of the Anglo-American efforts to 'reconstruct'the world which also led to the formation of the UN, GATT and, at a domestic level, the National Health Service. Bretton Woods led to the establishment of the system which bore its name. The exchange rate regime was to be one of flexible parities, a semi-fixed system, described above, p. 120. The parities were to be adjusted in the event of 'fundamental disequilibrium' after a process of international consultation. In practice, this was a dead letter and the 'efficient part' of Bretton Woods was an informal understanding that par values would not be changed very often nor without an effort to avoid the change. In other words devaluation would not be an 'easy' or 'costless' option. The system was often called the dollar exchange system, as the parities were set in terms of dollars. Although this convention was a reflection of US dominance, it paradoxically meant that the US could not devalue without breaking the system up.

International co-operation would be effected through two new institutions, the International Monetary Fund, IMF, and the International Bank for Reconstruction and Development, always known as the World Bank. As wags have always been fond of noting, the World Bank was a fund and the IMF a bank. The World Bank existed to make loans, on commercial terms, for development projects initially in Europe but later almost exclusively in the Third World. It has been very successful as has the soft-loan affiliate it spawned, the International Development Association, IDA. However as these two bodies are peripheral to the monetary system they will hereafter be ignored.

The IMF was also to serve as the body through whom loans were to be made. As the IMF is still of major importance, its structure and the peculiar mechanism by which it extends credit is described below in section 12.2. This system was established at the end of World War II. However, the practical workings of the system were dominated until 1957-8 by three related 'brute facts'.

12.1.1 American Dominance

This was the era of overwhelming US military supremacy and economic dominance. To a very considerable extent the US ran the world, with occasional assistance from Bevin over the Marshall plan, or deft obstruction from Attlee (Korea) or Eden (Indo-China) designed to avert war. The UK was still a major power but no other Western nation counted. The IMF has always reflected the reality of power, so it was in some sense a front-man for the US Treasury which provided the dollars it lent. The co-operation within the system was provided by American leadership and loans were, in effect, made by the US — whether through the Marshall plan and later variants, or the IMF.

12.1.2 The Dollar Shortage

This reflected (12.1.1); every nation but the US faced a balance of payments problem, or at least constraint, and the dollar was universally demanded and in short supply.

12.1.3 Restrictions on Transactions

This was a consequence of (12.1.2). Bretton Woods was supposed to involve convertibility of currencies, that is a French holder of sterling could change his pounds into dollars or marks. In practice even external convertibility was restricted until the late 1950s and savage restrictions on the movement of capital and goods were imposed — and enforced. In 1947 the US forced the UK government to make sterling convertible but the experiment was abandoned after five weeks and the ideal forgotten for a decade (see Worswick and Ady (1954) for the restrictions and the events of 1947 — chapters by Balogh (22), Sargent (23-4) and Ady (25) — and Dalton (1960) provides a detailed, vivid and illuminating description of the 'crisis' of 1947). These restrictions were associated with more restrictive policies on trade, see p. 30 above.

With a neatness rare in history all of these features disappeared in 1957-8 and a fundamentally different world monetary system arose. The US balance of payments swung into deficit on current account and the dollar shortage disappeared. The major European currencies all became convertible against the dollar and each other, at least for non-residents. In some places important steps towards convertibility had been taken earlier — e.g. the UK govenment's decision to support the transferable sterling exchange rate in 1955, but the major steps occurred in a brief period in 1957-8. US dominance did not disappear overnight but was slowly eroded by the reemergence of Germany under Adenauer, by growing Soviet might and by the steps taken towards a united Europe. Nevertheless, in 1957-8, the Russian sputnik dented US prestige; the EEC was founded and de Gaulle came to power in France, resolved to end American domination of Europe. In consequence central bank co-operation after 1957-8 was to take place against a background of conflicting interests and views between the US and continental Europe with a declining UK caught uneasily in the middle.

The major arguments arose over the persistent US and UK deficits. The dollar served as an international medium of exchange under Bretton Woods and sterling was still an international currency for historic reasons. Hence, US and UK current account deficits were financed by the creation of large quantities of dollars and pounds which the rest of the world had to accept. In effect as the creators of (international) money, the US (and to a lesser extent the UK) could behave like a domestic government. If it ran a deficit, this could be financed automatically by money creation. The consequence might be inflation but, whereas there are some checks on a government (e.g. elections), the German and French governments felt powerless to stem the flood of dollars and pounds.

The German-French complaints concerned the following.

12.1.4 Seignorage Profits

Money creation is highly profitable; a bank note costs about 5p to print but the issuer obtains goods in exchange worth, say, £10, depending on the note's denomination. This profit is called seignorage and, although the mechanism was complex, the US and UK benefited in a similar fashion. This especially irked the French as much of the seignorage profit was used to buy European assets. Authors grumbled about 'the American challenge' which would make American industry in Europe the world's third great power (Servan Schreiber (1969)). In essence, the French complaint was that the US was acquiring valuable assets in exchange for worthless pieces of paper and the UK was living beyond its income and settling its debts with worthless paper.

12.1.5 Inflation

In addition to the loss of real resources, the excess creation of liquidity led to inflation, see p. 158 above; or at least so the Franco-German group argued. The US and UK argued, of course, that unless they ran deficits liquidity would be inadequate so unemployment would rise.

However, the seignorage profits enjoyed by the US and UK were not costless. In principle they were liable to buy their liabilities back in either gold (for the US) or dollars (UK). Neither had anything like enough liquid assets to pay their liabilities. The US and UK had enjoyed bankers' profits but had avoided the bankers' responsibilities. The problem caused international tension when, in 1965, France announced its intention of refusing to increase its dollar holdings; any increase would be exchanged for gold at the $55 per ounce price fixed by President Roosevelt in 1935. The UK balance of current payments was in apparently permanent deficit, despite half-hearted deflation by the Wilson government in 1965-6. The US balance of payments was adversely affected by the Vietnam war from 1965 onwards. Finally, the growth of the Eurocurrency market was putting pressure on the adjustable parity system as the difficulty and the cost of maintaining fixed parities grew. However this was a minor factor until after 1968 (see below, p. 176).

Various 'band aids' were applied to the system. Large loans were extended to the UK who had to agree to repay in foreign currency; the end of seignorage profits. Large quantities of short-term sterling liabilities were in effect turned into medium-term foreign exchange liabilities by the Basle guarantees (see Blackaby (1976) especially p.3: 1-2 for details).

An ingenious scheme designed to solve several problems was the introduction of 'Special Drawing Rights', in 1967. These were linked in value to a so-called basket of currencies, an SDR is worth x cents and y pence and z pfennigs, etc. They were a form of international money created by the IMF and distributed amongst its members pro rata to their quotas, see below p. 169, approximately their wealth. This had various, inconsistent aspects to it:

1. Seignorage profits were distributed amongst all governments, not

restricted to two (US and UK), nor pre-empted by banks, as with Eurocurrency creation;

2. liquidity was increased, as the US and UK wanted;

3. SDRs were to *replace* dollars and sterling at least in part as the international medium of exchange.

(2) and (3) were apparently inconsistent, as some supporters believed they were increasing the quality of liquidity while others believed they were changing its composition with a view to reducing the total. If the IMF created world money, creation was expected to be less than if the US and UK created it.

These palliatives could not restore viability to the Bretton Woods system and it collapsed between 1967 and 1972. The collapse was marked by a series of events. First of all, the UK government was forced to devalue the pound in 1967. Then, in 1968, the London gold pool was suspended. This gold pool, supplied largely by the US, had kept the price of gold at $35 per ounce, the price fixed by Roosevelt. Thereafter, there was a free market price of gold which was to fluctuate wildly but was substantially higher than $35. The latter remained the official price (until it was raised to $42 in 1971) at which gold was valued in central banks' books. The official price became of less and less relevance throughout the 1970s. The devaluation of sterling and the suspension of the gold pool were body blows to the tottering Bretton Woods system but the knock-out punch was delivered by President Nixon in 1971. He announced a formal devaluation of the dollar which raised the official price of gold to $42 an ounce. More importantly his August measures (aptly called Nixon's Shokku by the Japanese) ended the system of semi-fixed exchange rates and introduced a period of dirty floating; convertibility of the dollar was suspended. An attempt was made to revive the Bretton Woods system by the Smithsonian agreement of December 1971, described by President Nixon as the 'greatest event in the history of the world'. This agreement produced a new set of parities and amended the Bretton Woods rules to permit fluctuations of 2 per cent on either side of the par values. The new scheme did not survive the UK government's decision to float in June 1972 and by March 1973 all the major currencies were floating. Henceforth, the exchange rate regime was to be one of dirty floating, modified by the regional schemes for adjustable parities of the EEC (see p. 173 below).

Attempts were to be made to restore adjustable parities during the 1970s. In particular a committee chaired by Sir Jeremy More proposed the 'Outline of Reform'. This proposed a 'wide bands' scheme of exchange rates which was effectively Bretton Woods with fluctuations of 10 per cent either side of parity rather than 1 per cent. This was rejected at the Kingston meeting of the IMF in 1976, because it was felt to incorporate the worst features of both Bretton Woods ('one-way options') and of 'dirty floating' (large short-term fluctuations). The committee had felt that it combined the flexibility of dirty floating with the advantages of fixed parities, not least for the IMF's internal workings.

The international monetary system had to adjust to the shock administered by OPEC's price increase of November 1973, see p. 6 above. The system required very little modification. IMF lending was expanded by the special facilities, discussed below, and by increasing 'quotas' so as to permit greater conventional lending, see below. The increased importance of the OPEC nations was recognised by an adjustment of power within OPEC. OPEC nations held very large balances with, mainly, New York and London banks. Some of these were 'Euro-currencies', i.e. external holdings, but they were mainly 'domestic deposits', i.e. dollars deposits with New York banks or sterling ones with UK banks. The only institutional change was a series of gold auctions which started in 1975. The IMF had run short of hard currencies and solved the problem by auctioning its gold (on one occasion in the late 1960s the IMF found that it had only Australian dollars and Venezuelan bolivars available). Gold auctions solved various problems an attracted diverse support, because

1. they expanded the IMF's liquid resources;
2. the US viewed it as a step towards demonetising gold;
3. because of (2), the IMF could realise its gold holdings held in New York without it seeming to show a lack of confidence in the US;
4. some European and Arab states thought the auctions increased the role of gold in the international monetary system – the IMF (and central banks) had not dealt in gold since 1968 – and moreover some of them wanted to buy, or let their citizens buy, the gold;
5. as the gold was on the IMF's books at $42 and was sold at market prices a profit ensued which was handed over to the IDA for lending to Third World countries; this received their support for the scheme;
6. the gold price was to some extent managed by the timing of the sales.

A large number of grandiose reforms were proposed in the late

1970s, all involving some combination of the gold standard, fixed parities, the creation of more SDRs (either to replace dollars already held or to increase Third World reserves or just to enable the IMF to lend more) and the creation of new international assets, often linked to commodity prices.

It seems safe to predict that nothing will come of them nor of any other reform ideas floated – such as the one proposed in September 1980. 'Dirty floating' and the so-called 'era of ad hoc' are here to stay.

12.2 Institutions

12.2.1 The IMF

The international monetary system is based upon 'dirty floating', but it remains to describe the institutional arrangements for co-operation and international lending. The IMF plays a key role under both heads. The IMF currently has over 140 member countries, comprising virtually all Western countries, most Third World countries and a few communist states such as Hungary. The internal organisation of and orthodox lending by the IMF is based on the quota assigned to each country. As each quota was originally fixed in terms of its own currency par values are needed to facilitate easy comparison and so that adjustments can be made at convenient intervals. Voting within the IMF is weighted by quota. For most decisions an 80 per cent majority is needed. This requirement gives the US a veto since its quota is over 20 per cent of the total. No other country at present has a veto, although the UK used to have one but various groups of countries can combine to block schemes. The IMF employs several thousand international civil servants headed by a managing director. They are supervised by a board of 20 directors, who are usually represented by deputies since the directors are either finance Ministers, such as the incumbent UK Chancellor, or central bank governors. The five largest quota holders have a director automatically. The big five have always included the US and the UK. Saudi Arabia is a recent entrant to this elevated status. The remaining members of the IMF are grouped into 15 blocs who each elect a director (invariably from the largest quota holder of the group) and an alternate from the second largest quota holder. This arrangement is remarkably stable; even when two members of a group are at war with each other the system operates smoothly.

Quotas are also the key to the IMF's conventional lending and the structured constraints placed upon nations in exchange for funds. Each nation was originally required to lodge a sum equal to its quota with the

IMF and to increase the deposit whenever its quota was increased. Twenty-five per cent of this must be paid in either gold or dollars, the remainder in one's own currency. In fact Switzerland paid all of its quota in gold and the US, of course, paid all of its in dollars, so the gold and dollar holding was over 25 per cent. A simplified case for a two-country IMF will be used; the two countries being A and B whose currencies are called αs and βs, 1α and 1β each being worth 1 dollar. A's quota is 100,000 so it pays over 75,000 αs and $25,000. Country B's quota is 200,000 so it subscribes 150,000 βs and $50,000. Hence the IMF holds 150,000 βs, 75,000 αs and $75,000.

Countries borrow from the IMF by making drawings, that is they exchange their currency for foreign currency. In the example B draws $10,000 and 20,000 αs giving 30,000 βs in exchange. The IMF now holds 55,000 αs, 180,000 βs and $65,000. The crucial calculation is: what is the IMF's holding of each currency as a percentage of the quota? In the example, the holding of A's currency is now 55 per cent of quota, B's 90 per cent. Once the percentage exceeds 75, the country is said to have drawn a tranche, these being divided into bands as follows:

75-100	gold tranche
100-125	first credit tranche
125-150	second credit tranche
150-175	third credit tranche
175-200	fourth credit tranche

IMF holdings of a member's currency are not allowed to exceed twice its quota. The gold tranche may be drawn without condition other than the payment of interest (currently 6¼ per cent) on the amount by which the holding exceeds 75 per cent of the quota. However, it is necessary to obtain IMF consent before each credit tranche is drawn. This is always conditional, the conditions being expressed in a 'letter of intent'.

Before discussing the nature of the conditions, two points are relevant to the working of the system. One is that the IMF obtains its funds interest free and earns two lots of interest on them. When the UK drew foreign exchange from the IMF in 1967 and 1977, the IMF received sterling which it invested (in Treasury bills) and in addition the UK paid interest because the IMF's holding of sterling exceeded its quota. In general the IMF charges interest on the currency it supplies but receives interest on the currency it receives in exchange. The other point is that most of the 'loans' are repaid by drawings by other nations. In 1969 New Zealand drew a large quantity of sterling from the IMF, thus repaying the UK's loan. In the example if at a later stage A draws 30,000 βs, in exchange for 30,000 αs, then IMF holdings of βs are now 85 per cent of A's quota but holdings of βs are down to 75 per cent of B's quota, so B's 'loan' has been repaid by A's transaction.

The conditions for a drawing are usually set out in a letter of intent. The conditions are usually stiffer as each successive tranche is drawn. These conditions vary considerably. In many cases a country has to agree to adhere to IMF rules, especially on convertibility and multiple exchange rates. IMF rules require that a currency be freely convertible at least for non-residents. Multiple exchange rates were invented by Schacht in Germany in the 1930s; he had over 300 of them. There are different rates for different transactions; a well-known one is the preferential rate available for tourists to Eastern Europe (preferential compared to the even less favourable official rate). The more publicised conditions concern domestic policy. Targets are invariably set for DCE and frequently for public spending or the PSBR, but never for monetary growth. Monitoring devices are used to see that these are met, ranging from a bi-annual visit to an adviser in the Prime Minister's office.

It is, however, necessary to emphasise the political reality behind these targets. They usually represent not scientific calculation by disinterested experts but the outcome of political bargaining. The IMF and the world financial system still reflect the nineteenth-century notions that the community of nations has a right to tell the individual nation what to do and that the view of the community reflects the view of the strong. The IMF reflects the reality of financial and economic power in a way that Palmeston would have understood. When the UK borrowed from the IMF in 1976, the crucial negotiations were those between the US and UK governments (the talks were prolonged because of the need to talk with the incoming (Carter) as well as outgoing (Ford) administrations). The very light conditions imposed on the UK reflected US policy, not the opinions of the international civil servants of the IMF. After the Portuguese revolution, Germany provided Portugal with funds and set the conditions, but it suited both Portugal and Germany to use the IMF as an intermediary. It is easier politically to say 'the IMF says we must raise taxes' than 'country X says we must'. It is also easier for the strong to use the IMF as a front-man. The IMF fulfils many useful functions but, like any body involving nation states, its functioning involves political processes.

Since 1973 the IMF has made a number of more straightforward

loans, that is, it has borrowed and lent without going through the rig-
marole of quotas, drawings and so on. The first such loans were the
'buffer stock' and oil facility of 1973. The latter was almost entirely
borrowed by the UK and Italy and was small ($1.3 billion) relative to
the deficits caused by OPEC price increases. The former was used only
to finance buffer stocks in tin and rubber. The largest was the Witeveen
facility, $16 billion, named after the then IMF managing director.
$16 billion was raised because no amount either smaller or larger could
be raised, as each country's contribution was conditional on others'
and only $16 billion satisfied all the conditions, or so the story went. At
the time of writing, Sir Geoffrey Howe was seeking to raise funds for
another such facility, in his capacity of chairman of the IMF.

12.2.2 The BIS

The Bank for International Settlements (BIS) is nominally a relic of
the interim arrangements established after World War I with such
picturesque quirks as shares which pay neither interest nor voting power
but are among the ultimate status symbols in the banking community.
In fact the institution acts as a forum for central bank co-operation
through the monthly meetings held in Basle. These arrange co-operative
acts in domestic and international policy, seeking a common reduction
in interest rates. On several occasions BIS meetings seem to have sought
to produce across the board interest rate reductions so as to stimulate
economies without changing exchange rates. BIS meetings frequently
arrange large loans. The UK government borrowed $3 billion in Novem-
ber 1964 and $5.2 billion in June 1976. Basle meetings arranged the
conversion of liquid sterling balances into illiquid foreign currency ones
in the late 1960s. The range and scope of action taken at BIS meetings
is enormous, but there are two major problems in describing it. One is
that the system is as informal and flexible as possible and one cannot
describe a structure that does not exist nor explain the rules of a body
without them. Moreover, the BIS is merely the agency of international
co-operation and in one sense one is recording the fact that central
bankers have co-operated since the 1920s to keep the international
monetary system functioning. Such co-operation is a vital part of the
system but by its nature not easily describable.

As an institution the BIS collects statistics and carries out research.
Its main corporate function, however, is that it manages the reserves of
some countries. By switching these from, say, US Treasury bills to bank
deposits or vice versa these have the effect of open-market operation on
the world banking system.

12.2.3 Swaps

Swaps, frequently arranged at BIS meetings, are a device whereby one central bank lends to another. The 'loan' is effected by an exchange of currencies, e.g. the Bundesbank giving the American 'Fed' DM 2 billion in exchange for $1 billion. These are prearranged so that a central bank knows that it has x billion available to supplement its reserves. The problem is that the lender risks monetary expansion when its currency is used to buy up some of the other currency, e.g. if in the above example the 'Fed' used its DM 2 billion to buy dollars to support the exchange rate, the effect would be an expansion of the German money supply. The 'swap' does nothing to diminish the costs of spot intervention, p. 152 above, but it may make it possible. Moreover, the use of 'swaps' involves an explicit decision about the cost of intervention. If, as in 1978, the Germans felt that the DM was overvalued against the dollar they could have intervened themselves. However, if they had they would have acquired dollars which they felt might depreciate in the medium term. An unsuccessful forward market intervention would have been even more costly. If the Germans supplied the US with marks by a swap and the US intervened, the US would bear these costs.

12.2.4 The EEC

The EEC has sought to produce a system of fixed parities amongst its members. This was intended to produce more integration amongst its members' economies but probably confuses ends and means and interferes with private sector integration – see Dosser, Gowland and Hartley (1982), pp. 19-20, 102-4. That exchange control between members has been introduced as a step towards union strikes all but the Euro-fanatic as bitterly ironical.

The first such scheme was the European Monetary Union, introduced in April 1972. This was to restrict movements of member and prospective member currencies to within 1¼ per cent of parity, about half the Smithsonian divergence (hence the name 'snake in the tunnel'). The UK left the system within six weeks and neither Italy nor Ireland joined. The French left the group in 1973 in all but name so the snake really became a DM bloc, reflecting German economic power and the dependence of economies like the Netherlands or Austria upon it (see p. 121 above).

In a triumph of political reality over economic sense, the EEC decided to try again in 1978. It has been argued that the consequent European Monetary System (EMS), which came into force on 1 January 1979, was an accident, in that d'Estaing, the French President, proposed it assuming that some one else would veto it. Certainly French participation was opposed by many French employers (CNPF) unions (CGT), bankers and economists. The EMS sought to restrict movements amongst the six full members (the EEC less the UK, Ireland and Italy) to within 3 per cent of parity and with the two associates (Ireland and Italy) to 6 per cent.

The system also included a European Currency Unit (ECU), which was equal to x centimes, y pence, z pfennigs, etc. (the proportions vary over time). A currency's rate against the ECU was calculated. If this fell out of line remedial domestic policy was required; e.g. in May 1979 Belgium was the first country whose currency fell below its ECU limit so it raised interest rates. The EMS also includes some reserve pooling, the Monetary Co-operation Fund. The EMS has been kept in existence only by frequent parity changes at great cost to its members, in that it provides 'one-way options' on occasion. It has achieved nothing except its survival as a token of co-operation. Its history has shown some amazing ironies. When the pound-punt (Irish pound) bank was broken on 1 January 1979, informed opinion was unanimous that the punt would rise against the pound and several billions of Irish securities had been bought by 'smart' investors to anticipate the gain. In fact within twelve months the punt had fallen 25 per cent. Problems had been caused for the EMS by an over-strong pound, whereas one reason the UK had not joined was a fear that the pound would be too weak to stay in.

12.3 The System in Action: A Case Study

This section presents a description of a particular episode in international monetary history designed to illustrate some of the points made in Chapters 9-11 about the impossibility of fixed parities and the problems faced by those who operate the international monetary system. Throughout 1976-8 the dollar was depreciating especially against the Swiss franc and the Deutschmark. At the end of 1975 the dollar was worth 2.62 Swiss francs and 2.65 DM, at the end of 1977 only 1.98 and 2.09 respectively. At the end of October it had fallen to 1.49 and 1.74, a loss of about 40 per cent of its value in under two years and 25 per cent in nine months. This fall reflected a mixture of lack of confidence in President Carter, fears about US oil imports and the US balance of payments deficit and a belief that Miller, the 'Fed' chairman, was expanding the US money supply too quickly. The German government, international opinion, reflected in the *Economist, The Times,*

Le Monde, etc, and Wall Street opinion, reflected in the *Wall Street Journal*, argued that President Carter should do something to defend the dollar. In particular the German authorities urged him to take action to transfer the costs of intervention to the US authorities; the Germans were buying dollars to hold the DM rate down but had no more confidence in the dollar than the speculators and did not wish to buy any more of this depreciating asset. The view was typical in its mixture of political and economic factors.

In November President Carter succumbed to the pressure, but it is much easier to see why he resisted earlier than why he gave in then. The cost of depreciation is mainly added inflationary pressure but this would be small, because its imports are so low relative to US GDP. Depreciation benefits producers, at the expense of consumers, and it is universally agreed that producers are much stronger than consumers in the US political system (see e.g. Cater (1965)). Finally the US had available only about $30 billion of short-term assets, $10 billion of foreign exchange and $20 billion of gold (not all of which could be sold for legal and practical reasons). It could borrow perhaps $30 billion, $20 billion of 'swaps' and $10 billion from the IMF, although this would have impaired the IMF's ability to lend to others. In November and December the 'swaps' were doubled to $40 billion. Against this, US short-term liabilities were $700 billion and another $600 billion of short-term claims were denominated in dollars in the Eurocurrency market and extra dollars could be created to sell to the US for harder currencies. Nevertheless Carter and Miller, by a mixture of borrowing and raising US interest rates, were to influence foreign exchange markets by a package of measures announced on 1 November; at the end of the month the dollar was worth 1.73 Swiss francs and DM 1.93. In 1979 the Soviet invasion of Afghanistan and the appointment of the monetarist Volcker to the 'Fed' were to have the effect of changing sentiment around so that the dollar became a very strong currency. The political dangers to Germany, let alone Switzerland, of a Soviet move against Afghanistan seemed remote to most readers of the *Guardian* but the desire for a safe haven in a troubled world is a major factor in foreign exchange markets. The foreign exchange market and the entire international financial system are a fascinating complex mixture of politics and economics. No student of international monetary theory, nor author of a textbook, should ever forget the nature of that which he or she seeks to analyse.

13 THE EUROCURRENCY MARKET

13.1 Introduction

There are two sorts of banking transaction, those carried out in the native currency and Euro ones. The dollar is the native currency in the USA, the pound in the UK and so on and traditionally nearly all banking transactions were executed in the respective native currency of the bank accepting a deposit. In recent years, however, more and more banking transactions have been Euro ones, that is involving banks in accepting deposits or making loans in a currency which is not native to them. A typical Eurocurrency transaction would involve an Arab depositing dollars with a London bank or an Italian borrowing Deutschmarks from a French bank. The precise definition of the Eurocurrency market has been a matter of some debate (see Gowland (1979), pp. 65-6) but the underlying concept is of an active banking market outside the country which issues the currency concerned. The Eurodollar market is the largest of the Euromarkets but there are Euromarkets in virtually all the European currencies. Many of the Eurobanks and dealing centres are located in Asia and currency never changes hands, so the name is potentially misleading.

There are two facts about the Eurocurrency market which dominate all analysis of it: its phenomenal size and incredible growth rate. In 1960 the market was about $2 billion. In 1980 it was about $1500 billion, including inter-bank transactions and $1100 billion net of them, i.e. there were $1500 billion of deposits in the market of which $1100 billion were held by firms, individuals and governments and $400 billion by banks. This is nine times the size of native currency banking business in the UK (on a comparable basis) and equal to 120 per cent of the US money supply.

The Euromarket is conventionally assumed to have been founded in 1927, although strictly medieval bankers were Eurobankers, but its period of phenomenal growth started with the changes in the world financial system in 1957-8 especially the end of the dollar shortage and the introduction of convertibility for European currencies (the history of the market involves major roles for Stalin, Hitler and, in some versions, the Mafia; for a detailed account, see Gowland (1979), pp. 69-72, for a brilliant, racy account Smith (1982)).

The nature of the market is such that it is almost totally beyond the control of any central bank, or any other official body. A transaction can be 'booked' in any country, so, for example, a German lending dollars to a Spaniard in London might record the transaction ('book' it) in Singapore; effectively all he would do is make the loan by giving the Spaniard a cheque drawn on a Singapore bank. Thus, attempts by any one country to control the market would merely push the market to another centre. No international body can, or is likely to, exercise control over banking, so the banks in the market are totally free of any prudential requirement. Moreover, banks in this market borrow short and lend long on a grand scale; in June 1982 only 15 per cent of deposits were for more than one year against 87 per cent of loans. All banks borrow short and lend long but rarely in so spectacular a fashion. Domestic banks are subject to various forms of control to minimise the risks they (and their depositors) run: licensing, ratios or deposit insurance (see Gowland (1978), pp. 97-101). In addition, central banks in practice accept a responsibility to cover the deficiency of any defaulting bank by one means or another. No such protection is available when a Eurobank crashes, e.g. the Bank Ambrosiano group collapse in 1982. The Italian authorities accepted a responsibility to protect the customers of its domestic banking business but not of its Eurobanking subsidiary (a Luxemburg company). Eurobanks have lent heavily to some sovereign borrowers whose repayment prospects are doubtful (Poland, Argentina). In practice, such debts have usually been rescheduled, i.e. the borrower is given longer to pay but the bank's balance sheet shows the asset as if it were beyond reproach.

In the mid-1970s, the conventional wisdom was that worries about the stability of the Eurobanks were misplaced, e.g. Crockett (1979), so the author's fears (Gowland (1979), p, 68) seemed alarmist in comparison. By 1982, orthodoxy had swung to the other extreme, and for example Mr Healey was not alone in his warning of a total collapse of the world banking system (*The Times*, 9 September 1982). By contrast, my views now seem almost Panglossian in their complacency. Nevertheless, it still seems to me (as in 1979, p. 68) that the system does not have the 'potential of a credit Anstalt to trigger a world depression (as was alleged to have happened in 1931) but it embodies considerable risks'. To deny the risk seems as foolhardy as it is ill-founded to produce apocalyptic visions of the collapse of the world financial order. In the second half of 1982, for example, careful management by the IMF and the US Federal Reserve System avoided the problems caused by a loss of confidence in the system. The costs included an easing of US monetary policy so the operation was neither costless nor impossible.

Many Eurobanks have been imprudent, but it may be that such risks are an inevitable byproduct of banking. The Eurobanks, like the domestic US banks, have proved very flexible and rendered the world great service in such activities as recycling OPEC surpluses, i.e. in accepting deposits from OPEC members and their citizens and on-lending them to those purchasing oil. The dangers arise from the absence of a central bank rather than the behaviour of the Eurobanks *per se*. Rather similar considerations apply as do to the analysis of US banks in the nineteenth century and Temin (1976) has argued that the costs imposed by unregulated banks and the occasional failure may not be as great as is conventionally assumed.

Finally, the Eurocurrency market is a very capitalistic institution, whether for good or ill. The Eurobanks normally put their responsibility to depositors and borrowers and the opportunity to earn profits far above adherence to the spirit of (national) government regulations. Often this means that the banks shelter the (rich) victims of oppression, as with the Jewish victims of Hitler in the market's early days. Sometimes criminals are sheltered but, much more importantly, facilities are provided to enable large companies to minimise tax or to evade exchange control. The market has probably been highly beneficial despite its drawbacks, but any analysis of it must acknowledge that it is capitalism, red in tooth and claw, with all its faces acceptable and otherwise.

13.2 Models of the Eurocurrency Market

Any model of banking has to start with the proposition that by lending a bank can create a deposit and that each loan must create a deposit (or equivalent liability of a bank) (Lipsey (1979), p. 378; Gowland (1982a), pp. 21-5). The basic problem is not to explain the growth of banks but to explain the limits to deposit creation. A naive student of elementary banking models might wonder why banks do not loan infinite amounts, despite the usual qualification about the difference between an individual bank and the banking sector. There are two basic approaches to this problem of explaining the constraints on loan and deposit creation; the multiplier approach and the profit maximisation approach, called the 'new view' of money, although it goes back at least a century to Bagehot and arguably to such fifteenth-century authors as the author of the *Mirror of Banking*. These explanations are the basis of alternative models of banking.

The 'multiplier' approach is based upon the idea that banks have to, or will be forced to choose to, maintain an approximately fixed proportion of reserves to deposits. Elementary textbooks often start with a seventeenth-century goldsmith who receives deposits in gold. He has to maintain, say, a 10 per cent reserve to meet repayments. Hence, if he gets a new deposit of £100 in gold he will retain £10 and loan out £90. The £90 is redeposited with him and he keeps £9 and loans £81, the £81 is redeposited and so on *ad infinitum.* In the end, his balance sheet shows liabilities of £1000, deposits, and assets of £1000 made up of £900 of loans and £100 of gold. The influx of £100 of gold has allowed a multiple expansion of deposits of the inverse of the reserve ratio (i.e. ten) times the inflow. Multiplier models extend this analysis in some ways, e.g. to allow leakages into other assets (Gowland (1982a), p. 59ff.). Nevertheless, the basic principle is retained, banks will behave in such a way that the total size of their assets (or deposits) will be in (more or less) fixed relationship to their holdings of reserve assets and that a change in the available quantity of reserve assets is both sufficient and necessary to explain changes in bank assets and loans. In some cases (Germany, the USA, Australia) the reserve holding is imposed by law but the multiplier school argue that even where legal restraints are missing, as in the Eurocurrency market, the banks will impose a ratio on themselves. In particular, this school has sought to explain the growth of Eurocurrency markets in this way by arguing that the balance of payments deficits, especially US ones, have provided the reserve assets which both permitted and caused growth.

The profit-maximising school of thought, to which the author belongs, believes that multiplier analysis is irrelevant to modern banking. Banks holdings of reserves will vary so much in both size and composition that there is no fundamental reserve ratio. It is true that banks must hold some cash but there is no fixed minimum, and the actual percentage is very low. Banks need only $1/4$ or $1/3$ per cent cash so the credit multiplier would vary between 300 and 400 and would be both unstable and move inversely with the size of deposits, so that there would be no relationship *at the margin* between deposits and reserves (in the elementary example above, the goldsmith might hold £100 of reserves, whether his deposits are £1000 (and the ratio 10 per cent) or £2000 (and the ratio 5 per cent)). Crucially to this approach, banks can always obtain reserve assets so it is *deposits which determine reserves, not vice versa.* The constraint upon banks is the balance sheet one that they must induce depositors to hold deposits equal to the size of their loans (less any owners' capital). Hence, what matters is the marginal cost of increasing deposits compared to the marginal revenue derived from increasing loans (marginal cost includes the cost of the necessary increase in reserves, if any) so multiplier analysis is a special case of the 'new view', where this cost is infinite. Of course, the theory can be extended from pure profit maximisation to include risk, managerial goals and so on. The 'new view' therefore explains the growth of the market by looking at the demand for loans and the supply of deposits and the exogenous factors which have shifted these schedules (e.g. US monetary policy in the 1960s, below, or the OPEC price increase of 1973). From these marginal cost curves and demand curves for the banking industry can be derived so output (i.e. deposits and loans) can be determined by using the usual apparatus of microeconomics, either competitive or monopolistic.

There has been a long debate about which of the two approaches is more relevant to the Eurocurrency market (see Makin's paper in Stem *et al.* (1976), pp. 357-62 for a brilliant summary of the early stages and Johnston (1981, 1982) for a later analysis). It is clear that the argument will have to be resolved empirically since *a priori* either might be right. Friedman and Schwartz (1963) showed conclusively that the US banking system could be explained by multiplier analysis prior to 1914 whereas Goodhart (1972) showed that, in the same period, the UK system could not. Indeed, the UK banking system has never been explicable by multiplier analysis, see Gowland (1982a) pp. 11-12 and Chapter 3. Plausibility and the currently available evidence suggests that the 'new view' is right, but the debate is not over yet.

In any case it is necessary to explain the inter-relationship between domestic and Euro-banking. Both schools of thought can do this but the analysis is less awkward with the 'new view'. All Eurocurrencies are perfect substitutes for each other, because as the interest parity theory holds in this market so one can always invest in a deposit in currency A directly or indirectly via a deposit in currency B and a forward purchase of A for B and receive the same return. Domestic and Euro-deposits of the same currency are substitutes for each other and so are loans. Hence, the cost of borrowing in the US is one of the factors determining the demand for Eurodollar loans — just as the price of raspberry jam is a factor explaining the demand for strawberry jam. Similarly the return on domestic dollars influences the desire to hold Eurodollar deposits. In the 1960s, this substitutability was the main factor determining the growth of the market since the US authorities both restricted the rate of interest paid on bank deposits in the US (regulation Q), thereby making Eurodollar deposits more attractive and forced a lot of borrowers from the US domestic market to the Euromarket (see Gowland (1979), pp. 70-1 for details). Faced with a simultaneous rightward shift of both the marginal cost curve, because of the former, and marginal revenue curve, the market grew. As Euro- and domestic markets are always substitutes, the growth of the Euromarkets has served to integrate world money markets.

To summarise this section, there are two alternative theories of the Eurocurrency market; the multiplier approach and the profit maximisation or 'new view' model. The role of reserve assets is debatable but it is clear that the 'new view' is right in emphasising the adaptability of banks in grasping various opportunities presented to them by chance or official blunders over the years. The story of the market shows innovative capitalism in its most striking form.

13.3 The Impact of a Unified Capital Market

To a very large extent the growth of the Eurocurrency market has integrated the world's money and credit markets. The most immediate impact of this has been to increase competition in banking throughout the world. In the 1950s banking was a cartelised industry with small groups dominating the industry in each country (or region, in the USA), usually working in close accord with the relevant central bank. The desire of each cartel to raid the others, and willingess of members of a cartel to compete abroad but not at home, was a major cause of the growth of Eurocurrency business. Equally, however, the growth of Eurocurrency business has played a large role in smashing the cosy cartels of the 1950s. The change is most marked in wholesale business (large transactions) but there is now much more competition even in retail business than in the 1950s.

The integration of banking has had a large effect upon all industry and services. More or less, all large firms compete in the same market for funds and can invest their spare resources in the same market. It is difficult to overstate the role of the integration of banking in integrating economic activity more widely. It is impossible to isolate the role of Eurocurrency markets from that of cheaper transport and trade liberalisation in promoting a more unified world economy since 1950 but the effect of banking has not been the least of the factors involved. Moreover, a substantial percentage of world trade is financed by Eurocurrency market transactions (see Gowland (1979), p. 68).

The effect of the growth of Eurocurrency markets on economic policy has been pervasive but not particularly uniform. The *simpliste* argument is that an integrated financial system will deprive a nation of any autonomy in the conduct of its monetary policy. This argument is based upon a presumption of almost perfectly elastic capital flows with respect to interest rate changes, so if the authorities seek to change interest rates they will be unable to do so as the rest of the world creates the open economy equivalent of a horizontal LM curve which pegs the interest rate at the world level. If the target is a monetary one, similar problems apply because, although the authorities can change DCE, the change in DCE will involve a change in interest rates which will induce a capital flow, such that the overseas impact on the money supply exactly offsets the effect of the change in DCE. Direct controls, such as credit ceilings, can be circumvented by Eurocurrency trans-actions, as in Italy in 1969-70. More sophisticated analyses qualify this by pointing out that the argument implicitly assumes a constant ex-change rate. Otherwise it is possible to control the money supply, or the interest rate, so long as the exchange rate is allowed to adjust to the appropriate level. For example, a higher interest rate can be maintained so long as the exchange rate is so high that is is expected to fall by the amount of the differential (i.e. if dollar rates are 10 per cent, sterling rates can be 15 per cent if and only if the pound's value in terms of dollars is so high that is is expected to fall by 5 per cent so as to equate the return measured in dollars from both currencies). Hence, the standard conclusion, e.g. derived in Mundell (1968), is that if capital markets are integrated (perfect capital mobility) then a government can control any one of the money supply, the exchange rate and the rate of interest, but only one of them. The UK government in 1977-8 and 1979-81 seemed to face this choice and resolved to control the money supply (see Gowland (1982a), pp.160 and 190).

The theoretical answer to the dilemma for a government wishing to control both money and exchange rates is Keynes's solution discussed above, p. 124. This is to use forward market operations so as to control both the exchange rate and a domestic target (money or interest rates). However, this is not practicable because of the enormous scale on which forward contracts might have to be extended and the consequent scale of possible losses. The alternative answer is to insulate the domestic economy from the market by (both inward and outward) ex-change control. This was advocated by the UK House of Commons Treasury Committee in 1980 but has been successfully used only by the German authorities with the Bardepot. This, when imposed, required any German firms or individuals borrowing from abroad (i.e. including a bank taking a deposit) to lodge any percentage specified by the Bundesbank with the Bundesbank at an interest rate of the Bundesbank's choice. The sting of this device is the negative interest rate — down to minus 10 per cent. Ruthless enforcement enabled the German authorities to use this device to insulate the domestic mark banking market from the Euromarkets. This sort of exchange control requires a political will and availability of means of enforcement that few governments possess. Another fundamental effect of the Eurocurrency market on economic policy is that a nation with a balance of payments deficit need no longer deflate (see Gowland (1979), p. 72).

The sheer size of the Eurocurrency market has meant that fixed exchange rates of the Bretton Woods type can no longer be maintained, see p. 130 above. The consequences of the change to dirty floating are as far reaching as they are incalculable. One is that world inflation has probably been higher than it would otherwise have been. If this is so, it has reinforced the direct inflationary effects of the market. These arise because the Eurocurrency has caused, or at least been the agent of, a massive expansion of world credit money and liquidity. In this way, the Eurocurrency market has had an immense effect upon the world but it has been so pervasive that it is impossible to isolate its effects. Indeed, it is, in principle, impossible, since it is necessary to know how central banks and governments would have acted in the absence of the market. Otherwise it cannot be determined whether Eurodeposits and loans have been additional to, or replacements for, domestic ones.

To conclude, analysis of the Euromarkets puts the economist in the position of a historian in 1500 trying to assess the significance of Columbus's discovery of America. It is clearly very important, but it is not yet clear exactly why nor what the future effects will be.

A GUIDE TO FURTHER READING

There are three excellent advanced textbooks which can be recommended. In approximately ascending order of complexity, these are Sodersten (1980), Kindelberger and Lindert (1978) and Grubel (1977). In addition, there are a number of useful specialist textbooks: Findlay (1971), Shone (1972) (pure theory), Michaely (1977) (commercial policy) and Crockett (1979) (international finance). References to these are omitted below.

Pure Theory (Chapter 2)

Clement *et al.* (1967) sets out the issues comprehensively. Johnson (1958) is still a very useful guide to the complexities of the subject, as is Pearce (1970, Book II). Batra (1973), Chapters 3 to 5, is very difficult but even more rewarding.

Commercial Policy (Chapters 3 and 4)

Johnson (1971) is extremely comprehensive. On specific topics the following are recommended: Batra (1973), Chapter 9, on the effective rate of protection; Bhagwati (1969) on the effect of protection on producers' incomes; Bhagwati and Ramaswami (1963) on domestic monopoly; Falvey (1975) on tariffs and quotas.

Customs Unions (Chapter 5)

Krauss (1972) is a superb survey article which explores most of the literature and puts it into context. Robson (1972) is a well-chosen collection of articles, including the classic Viner (1950), Lipsey (1957a) and Cooper and Massell (1965a). Lipsey (1970) and El-Agraa and Jones (1981) provide comprehensive surveys for the mathematically oriented. Those interested specifically in the EEC should consult Swann (1978), Dosser *et al.* (1982) and El-Agraa (1980) in approximately ascending order of complexity.

Balance of Payments Theory (Chapters 6 to 8)

On the conceptual and statistical material, the (annual) *Guide to the Official Statistics* published by the CSO lists a huge range of sources and explains what the official statistics are. However, the annual *UK Balance of Payments*, HMSO, presents all the major items and explains their meaning. The best summary of the orthodox theory is still Haberler's paper, reprinted in Cooper (1969), pp. 107-34.

The best summary of the Keynesian approach is Johnson, reproduced in Cooper (1969), pp. 237-56 and in Frenkel and Johnson (1976), pp. 46-64. Mundell's model can be found in Mundell (1968) along with many other extensions of his approach. Chapter 8 (also in Frenkel and Johnson (1976), pp. 64-92) is an alternative open economy IS-LM model to the one above. The standard exposition of New Cambridge is by Cripps and Godley (1976); for further analyses see Gowland (1982b), pp. 71-6, Crystal (1979) and Cuthbertson (1979). For the overseas impact on the money supply see Gowland (1982a), pp. 43-9.

The standard exposition of the monetary approach is Frenkel and Johnson's compilation (1976); of especial value are Chapters 6 and 11 (by Johnson) and the introductory piece by the editors. At a more advanced level Dornbusch (1980) is the best available presentation of what is a moderate or modified monetarist stance. A relatively simple sympathetic presentation is by Crystal (1979) and a comparable, more hostile analysis is Cuthbertson (1979). Hahn (1977) and Currie (1976) contain criticism at a much more advanced level.

Exchange Rates (Chapters 9 and 10)

The best piece upon the merits of fixed and floating rates is the debate between Friedman and Roosa (1967). Johnson (1969) is still a classic if polemical piece. For those who prefer an attempt at balanced judgement to elegant advocacy, Gowland (1979), Chapter 2 is available.

The effect of the exchange rate on the economy is considered briefly in many places but rarely comprehensively. Mundell (1968) and Rhomberg (1978) are perhaps the best available.

International Finance (Chapter 11)

Williamson (1973) is a first-class summary of the international liquidity literature. Grubel's survey article (1971) is an ideal complement to it.

The International Monetary System (Chapter 12)

Gold (1970) is a first-rate guide to the IMF. The history of the international monetary system is reviewed in several excellent books of which Tew (1982) is perhaps the best.

The Eurocurrency Market (Chapter 13)

Crockett (1979), Chapter 12, and Gowland (1979), Chapter 3, provide useful introductions to the Eurocurrency market. Stem *et al.* (1976) is still the best available advanced material together with Johnston (1983) and Dreyer (1980).

BIBLIOGRAPHY

'Adam Smith' (Goodman, G.J.W.) (1982) *Paper Money* (UK edition), Macdonald, London

Balassa, B. (1963) 'An Empirical Determination of Classical Comparative Cost Theory', *Review of Economics and Statistics*, vol. 37 (August)

Baldwin, R.E. (1971a) *Non-Tariff Distortions on International Trade*, Brookings Institution, Washington DC

Baldwin, R.E. (1971b) 'Determinants of the Commodity Structure of US Trade', *American Economic Review*, vol.61 (March)

Bank (1979) *Bank of England Model of the UK Economy*, Bank of England Discussion Paper No.5 (September)

Batra, R.N. (1973) *Studies in the Pure Theory of International Trade*, Macmillan, London

Batra, R.N. (1975) *The Pure Theory of International Trade under Uncertainty*, Macmillan, London

Beckerman, W. (ed.) (1972) *The Labour Government's Economic Record 1964-70*, Duckworth, London

Bhagwati, J.N. (1959) 'Protection, Wages and Real Income', *Economic Journal*, vol. 69, pp. 733-44

Bhagwati, J.N. (1969) *International Trade: Selected Readings*, Penguin, Harmondsworth

Bhagwati, J.N. (1971) 'Customs Unions and Welfare Improvement', *Economic Journal*, vol. 81 (September), pp. 580-7

Bhagwati, J.N. and Ramaswami, V.K. (1963) 'Domestic distortions, tariffs and the theory of optimum subsidy', *Journal of Political Economy*, vol. 71

Blackaby, F.T. *et al.* (1978) *British Economic Policy 1960-74*, Cambridge University Press, Cambridge

Buchanan, J.M. and Brennan, H.G. (1981) 'Monopoly in Money and Inflation', *Hobart Paper 88*, Institute of Economic Affairs

Buchanan, N.S. (1955) 'Lines on the Leontief Paradox', *Economica Internazionale*, vol. 8 (November), p. 791

Cater, D. (1965) *Power in Washington* (English edition), Collins, London

Claasen, E.M. and Salin, P. (1976) *Recent Issues in Monetary Economics*, North Holland, New York

Clark, P.B. (1970) 'Demand for International Reserves: A Cross-country Analysis', *Canadian Journal of Economics*, vol. 3 (November), pp. 577-94

Clement, M.O., Pfister, F.L. and Rothwell, K.J. (1961) *Theoretical Issues in International Economics*, Houghton Miflin, New York

Cooper, C.A. and Massell, B.F. (1965a) 'Towards a General Theory of Customs Unions for Developing Countries', *Journal of Political Economy*, vol. 73, pp. 461-76

Cooper, C.A. and Massell, B.F. (1965b) 'A New Look at Customs Union Theory', *Economic Journal*, vol. 75 (December), pp. 742-7

Cooper, R.N. (ed.) (1969) *International Finance*, Penguin, Harmondsworth

Cripps, T.F. and Godley, W.A.H. (1976) 'A Formal Analysis of the CEPG Model', *Economica*, vol. 43 (November)

Crockett, A.D. (1979) *International Money*, Nelson, London

Crystal, K.A. (1979) *Controversies in British Macroeconomics*, Philip Allan, Oxford

Currie, D.A. (1976) 'Some Criticisms of the Monetary Analysis of Balance of
    Payments Correction', *Economic Journal*, vol. 86 (September), pp. 508-22
Cuthbertson, K. (1979) *Macroeconomic Policy*, Macmillan, London
Dalton, H. (1962) *High Tide and After: Memoirs 1945-60*, Muller, London
Dam, K.W. (1970) *The GATT*, University of Chicago Press, Chicago
Dornbusch, R. (1980) *Open Economy Macroeconomics*, Basic Books, New York
Dosser, D., Gowland, D.H. and Hartley, K. (1982) *Collaboration amongst
    Nations*, Martin Robertson, Oxford
Dreyer, J.S., Haberler, G. and Willett, T.D. (eds.) (1980) *The International
    Monetary System: A Time of Turbulence*, American Enterprise Institute for
    Public Policy Research, Washington and London
El-Agraa, A.M. (1980) *The Economics of the European Community*, Philip Allan,
    Oxford
El-Agraa, A.M. and Jones, A.J. (1981) *The Theory of Customs Unions*, Philip
    Allan, Oxford
Ellis, H.S. and Meltzer, L.A. (eds.) (1949) *Readings in the Theory of Interna-
    tional Trade*, Irwin, Homewood, Illinois
Falvey, J.F. (1975) 'A Note on the Distinction between Tariffs and Quotas',
    Economica, vol. 42 (August), pp. 319-26
Findlay, R. (1970) *Trade and Specialization*, Penguin, Harmondsworth
Frenkel, J.A. and Johnson, H.G. (eds.) (1976) *The Monetary Approach to the
    Balance of Payments*, George Allen and Unwin, London
Friedman, M. (1953) 'The Case for Flexible Exchange Rates' in *Essays in Positive
    Economics*, University of Chicago Press, Chicago
Friedman, M. and Roosa, R.V. (1967) *Balance of Payments: Free versus Fixed
    Exchange Rates*, Rational Debate Seminars, American Enterprise Institute,
    Washington DC
Friedman, M. and Schwartz, A.J. (1963) *A Monetary History of the US 1867-
    1960*, NBER Studies in Business Cycles No. 12, Princeton University Press,
    Princeton
Galbraith, J.K. (1954) *The Great Crash* (English edition), Hamish Hamilton,
    London (also published by Pelican (1961))
Gehrels, F. (1956) 'Customs Unions from a Single Country Viewpoint', *Review of
    Economic Studies*, vol. 34,pp. 61-4
Glyn, A. and Sutcliffe, R.B. (1972) *British Capitalism, Workers and the Profit
    Squeeze*, Penguin, Harmondsworth
Godley, W.A.H. *et al*. (1980) 'Britain and Europe', *Cambridge Economic Policy
    Review*, vol. 6 (April), pp. 27-34
Godley, W.A.H. *et al*. (1981) 'The European Community: Problems and
    Prospects', *Cambridge Economic Policy Review*, vol. 7 (December)
Gold, J. (1970) *The Stand-by Arrangements of the International Monetary Fund:
    A Commentary on their Formal Legal and Financial Aspects*, IMF, Washington
    DC
Goodhart, C.A.E. (1972) *The Business of Banking 1891-1914*, Weidenfeld and
    Nicholson, London
Gould, B., Mills, J. and Stewart, S. (1981) *Monetarism or Prosperity*, Macmillan,
    London
Gowland, D.H. (1978) *Monetary Policy and Credit Control*, Croom Helm,
    London
Gowland, D.H. (ed.) (1979) *Modern Economic Analysis*, Butterworth, London
Gowland, D.H. (1982a) *Controlling the Money Supply*, Croom Helm, London
Gowland, D.H. (ed.) (1982b) *Modern Economic Analysis 2*, Butterworth,
    London
Gowland, D.H. and Pakenham, K. (1974) 'Floating Rates and Inflation', *RIB*

Monthly Review (November)

Grubel, H.G. (1971) 'The Demand for International Reserves: A Critical Review of the Literature', *Journal of Economic Literature*, vol. 13 (December)

Grubel, H.G. (1976) *The International Monetary System*, Penguin, Harmondsworth

Grubel, H.G. (1977) *International Economics*, Irwin, Homewood, Illinois

Hahn, S.H. (1977) 'The Monetary Approach to the Balance of Payments', *Journal of International Economics*, vol. 7 (August)

Hartley, K. (1982) *Nato Arms Cooperation*, George Allen and Unwin, London

Henderson, P.D. (1968) 'Investment Criteria for Public Enterprise' in R. Turvey (ed.) *Public Enterprise*, Penguin, Harmondsworth

Hirst, F.W. (1911) *The Stock Exchange*, Williams and Northgate, London

Johnson, H.G. (1958) *International Trade and Economic Growth*, Unwin University Books

Johnson, H.G. (1969) 'The Case for Flexible Exchange Rates, 1969' in 'UK and Floating Exchanges', *Hobart Paper 46*, Institute of Economic Affairs

Johnson, H.G. (1971) *Aspects of the Theory of Tariffs*, George Allen and Unwin, London

Johnston, R.B. (1980) *Banks' International Lending Decisions and the Determination of Spreads on Syndicated Medium-term Euro-credits*, Bank of England Discussion Paper No. 12 (September)

Johnston, R.B. (1981) Theories of the Growth of the Euro-Currency Market: A Review of the Euro-Currency Deposit Multiplier', *BIS Economic Papers No. 4* (May)

Johnston, R.B. (1983) *The Economics of the Euro-Market*, Macmillan, London

Kemp, M.C. (1976) *Three Topics in the Theory of International Trade*, North Holland, Amsterdam

Keynes, J.M. (1971) *A Tract on Monetary Reform*, reprinted in *The Collected Writings*, Macmillan for the RES, 1971

Kindelberger, C.P and Lindert, P.H. (1978) *International Economics*, (sixth edition), Irwin, Homewood, Illinois

Krauss, M.B. (1972) 'Recent Developments in Customs Union Theory', *Journal of Economic Literature*, vol. X, no. 2 (June), pp. 413-35

Kuska, A.E. (1972) 'The Pure Theory of Devaluation', *Economica*, vol. 49

Laidler, D.E.W. and Parkin, J.M. (1975) 'Inflation – a Survey', *Economic Journal*, vol. 85 (December)

Leontief, W. (1956) 'Factor Proportions and the Structure of American Trade: Further Theoretical and Empirical Analysis', *Review of Economics and Statistics*, vol. 31 (November)

Leontief, W. (1969) 'Domestic Production and Foreign Trade: The American Position Re-examined' in J. Bhagwati (ed.) *International Trade*, pp. 93-139, Penguin, Harmondsworth

Lipsey, R.G. (1957a) 'Mr Gehrels on Customs Unions', *Review of Economic Studies*, vol. 34, no. 65, pp. 211-14

Lipsey, R.G. (1957b) 'The Theory of Customs Unions:Trade Diversion and Welfare', *Economica*, vol. 34, pp. 40-46

Lipsey, R.G. (1960), 'The Theory of Customs Unions: A General Survey', *Economic Journal*, vol. 70, pp. 496-513

Lipsey, R.G. (1970) *The Theory of Customs Unions: A General Equilibrium Analysis*, Weidenfeld and Nicholson, London

Lipsey, R.G. (1979) *An Introduction to Positive Economics* (fifth edition), Weidenfeld and Nicholson, London

Lipsey,R.G. and Lancaster, K.J. (1956) 'The General Theory of the Second Best', *Review of Economic Studies* XXXIV, vol. 63 (October), pp. 11-32

Loeb, G.A. (1954) 'A Estrutura do Comércio Exterior da América do Norte', *Revista Brasileira de Economia*, vol. 8 (December), p. 81

MacDougall, G.D.A. (1951-2) 'British and American Exports:A Study Suggested by the Theory of Comparative Costs', *Economic Journal*, vol. 61 (December 1951) and vol. 62 (September 1952)

Machup, F. (1969) 'The Cloakroom Rule of International Reserves', *Quarterly Journal of Economics*, vol. 79, pp. 337-55

Melvin, J. (1969) 'Comments on the Theory of Customs Unions', *Manchester School*, vol. 36, no. 2 (June), p. 161-8

Metzler, L. (1949) 'Tariffs, the Terms of Trade and the Distribution of Income', *Journal of Political Economy*, vol. 57 (February)

Michaely, M. (1977) *Theory of Commercial Policy*, Philip Allan, Oxford

Mundell, R.A. (1968) *International Economics*, Macmillan, New York

Oulton, N. (1973) *Tariffs, Taxes and Trade in the UK: The Effective Protection Approach*, HMSO, London

Pearce, I.F. (1970) *International Trade*, Papermac (Macmillan), London

Rhomberg, A. (ed.) (1978) *The Monetary Approach to the Balance of Payments*, IMF, Washington DC

Robson, P. (ed.) (1972) *International Economic Integration*, Penguin, Harmondsworth

Rueff, J. (1967) *Balance of Payments*, Macmillan, London

Samuelson, P.A. (1948) 'International Trade and the Equalisation of Factor Prices', *Economic Journal*, vol. 58 (June)

Samuelson, P.A. (1966) *Economics* (11th edition), McGraw Hill, New York

Servan Schreiber, J.J. (1969) *The American Challenge*, Avon Books, New York

Shone, R. (1972) *The Pure Theory of International Trade*, Macmillan, London

Shoup, C.P. (ed.) (1967) *Fiscal Harmonisation in Common Markets*, Columbia University Press, New York

Sodersten, B. (1980) *International Economics*, Macmillan, London

Sohmen, E. (1969) *Flexible Exchange Rates*, University of Chicago Press, Chicago

Stem, C.H., Makin, J.H. and Logue, D.E. (eds.) (1976) *Eurocurrencies and the International Monetary System*, American Enterprise Institute, Washington DC

Stern, R.M. (1962) 'British and American Productivity and Comparative Costs in International Trade', *Oxford Economic Papers* (October)

Stern, R.M. (1973) *The Balance of Payments*, Macmillan, London

Stolper, W.F. and Samuelson, P. (1941) 'Protection and Real Wages', *Review of Economic Studies*, vol. 9, pp. 58-73

Swann, D. (1978) *The Economics of the Common Market* (4th edition), Penguin, Harmondsworth

Swerling, B.C. (1954) 'Capital Shortage and Labor Surplus in the United States', *Review of Economics and Statistics*, vol. 36 (August), p. 286

Temin, P. (1976) *Did Monetary Forces Cause the Great Depression?*, Norton, New York

Tew, B. (1982) *The Evolution of the International Monetary System 1945-81*, Hutchinson, London

Viner, J. (1950) *The Customs Union Issue*, Carnegie Endowment for International Peace, New York

Williams, P.M. (1971) *Politics and Society in de Gaulle's Republic*, Longman, London

Williamson, J.H. (1973) 'Surveys in Applied Economics: International Liquidity', *Economic Journal*, vol. 83 (September)

Williamson, J.H., Wood, G.E. and Carse, S. (1980) *The Financing Procedures of British Foreign Trade*, Cambridge University Press, Cambridge

Worswick, G.D.N. and Ady, P.A. (eds.) (1952) *The British Economy*, Oxford University Press, Oxford

INDEX